The Stoic Salesperson

Acknowledgements

This book would've never happened without the challenge issued to me by James Altucher on his podcast. It's awesome to have people in your life who push you to do better. He's a great man, kind, supportive, and intelligent. Thanks for pushing me to put this into the world, James.

Check out the podcast here: https://youtu.be/Z-QIQQQBfN8, or by looking up "James Altucher 30 day book challenge" on YouTube.

The Stoic Salesperson

By Brendon "Be No Friend to Rome" Lemon

TABLE OF CONTENTS

Table of Contents

PART ONE
INTRODUCTION

Why Stoicism for Sales?

The most popular genre of anything is true crime. Just accept that as a fact.

This book would probably become a best seller if it was "True Crime and Sales" or "Lessons from the best serial killers on how to make money in sales." It's just true. For some reason, all of us sitting in our normal, unexciting lives really, really love true crime. Probably it's because it gives us something exciting to think about and reminds us the world is still dangerous. Most of us wake up, go through the motions, and head back to bed to do it again tomorrow. Then, every once in a while, somebody gets murdered.

I have a theory that part of the reason true crime is so interesting to so many is because it's one of the few times that we are starkly reminded that "*You are not really in control of your life.*" It's a weird kind of paradox that most of us like to ride: we like to feel safe and believe that we can control what happens to us.

Not true.

Not even a little bit.

True crime reminds us of this.

A divorcee meets a man on a dating site, a doctor, and they hit it off in a whirlwind romance. In a little over two months, despite the misgivings of her family, they were married. Over the next few months she learns that he isn't a doctor. Not only isn't he a doctor, he's broke. Not only is he broke, he had gotten out of prison only days before they went on that first date. Turns out, he wants her money. It's a nightmare.

She learns he's a sociopath, vindictive, and bent on destroying her life if she leaves him. He has multiple restraining orders out against him from women he's done this to in the past. Finally, she pushes him

3

out of her life and seeks legal action. Pushed to the edge, he assaults her daughter in the parking lot of her apartment building, stabbing and nearly killing her. She manages to wrestle the knife away from him and buries the knife deep into his eye socket.

In the hospital, his visiting sister arrives to find him in a coma and tells the doctors to pull the plug. Good riddance.

Evil exists, apparently.

This was a real story that happened to real people. The world is chaos.

Every day we wake up and wade out into it. And over time, years and years, we've all developed ways to cope. Mostly, it's by believing that we can control things.

Until I was in my late 20s, every relationship I was in was essentially based on anxiety. I was constantly afraid the object of my affection didn't love me back, wasn't as interested, or was about to end the relationship. Once when I was a senior in college this happened particularly badly. I lied awake at night scheming on how to keep her affections. It occupied all of my thought. Incapacitated with worry, I would go over every scenario that could possibly happen again and again in my mind. I tried to come up with contingency plans for everything. Ultimately, what I was trying to do was to *control* the other player in this game.

This is a surefire recipe for disaster on every front, but definitely in the world of romance. Of course this relationship ended.

When it did I experienced a roller-coaster of emotions. I got depressed for feeling powerless, angry that the actions I took didn't work, ashamed that I wasn't powerful enough a man to have a woman never question leaving me. All the normal fodder that idiot boys wrangle their way through when romance doesn't go their way. It hurt. It took me a long time to recover.

In my first successful relationship I took the mentality "Yeah, she's great and I like her, we'll see what happens." I just let go of trying to control anyone or anything. I let her make her own decisions. We fell in love and it's the healthiest relationship I've ever been in.

When I first joined the world of sales, I also went on a roller coaster. I would scheme, stay up late worried about how I was going to hit my number, and generally have complete terror at the thought of what the future held. Maybe you relate to this, I have a feeling that most salespeople do.

Just like that college relationship, I would stay up late thinking about what actions I could take. What could I say that would influence the prospect so completely that they'd have to buy. Without knowing it I was right there again in the throes of believing I could control the other player in the game. Just like you'd expect, things tended not to go well.

I would lose deals left and right. It was awful. I was a wreck. Eventually I quit my sales job, quit trying to date anyone, and moved to France where I basically bummed around for six months. There, I read almost all the time and finally discovered a book called The Enchiridion by Epictetus. This was my first source of stoicism.

I'd heard the word before, I was a philosophy major in college (it's amazing *any* woman was interested). Strangely though, we'd never studied it. Turns out that most philosophy students don't. Hardly anyone really teaches or learns it.

It's hard to overestimate how much this book changed my life. I went from anxious, frustrated, and depressed about my inability to control things in my life to understanding, accepting and surrendering to the things I can't control. Suddenly, without wasting energy on things I couldn't make better, I was able to focus on the things I *could* make better. My relationships improved. My sales improved. I became manager of the team. I stopped losing sleep. It really did feel like I found a kind of magic bullet.

Pouring into stoic philosophy, I found passages that could apply to my everyday on the sales floor. How to deal with prospects, how to manage myself and my emotions. How to maintain a mindset and demeanor that attracted sales to me; the words of ancient wise men proved the greatest foundation to build a sales career on. It made sense. The world is chaos.

Every day on the sales floor, salespeople confront chaos they mistakenly believe they can control. They make decisions about what lies inside or outside their locus of control without ever being aware that they're making them. They mistakenly believe they have more power than they do, and consequently their strategies fail because they cannot control critical elements of those strategies. Because of this fundamental mistake, many salespeople continuously find themselves in a vicious cycle of ambitious desire to make or beat their number, lots of effort at faulty plans, and then disappointment, anger, and depression when those plans don't work out.

Even more tragic, many sales team leaders simply don't understand this basic distinction either and as a result can't manage others through it. The head of sales at one large firm where I once worked had a career marked by sales won during a growing economy and an industry-wide technological shift *toward* the technology he was selling. It's probably easy to make a fundamental attribution error in this circumstance and believe it was *you* who made all those sales happen. In this organization, the leadership team perhaps all mistakenly believed that the successes of their early to mid careers was due predominantly to their ability to control and influence prospects to buy. Consequently, they emphasized the role of the salesperson *over* other factors. When the sales team wasn't performing, they tended to blame the salespeople, or worse, throw their hands up.

Not a lot of really novel ideas came out of that leadership group. We kept missing our numbers, things got bad. Flash forward a few years and everybody has quit and moved on to other positions.

A lot of good salespeople got a whole lot of nothing done because of this fundamental attribution error. They lost time. They lost sales. They easily sacrificed opportunities in their respective careers because they trusted a team that had a track record of success, only to learn that whatever magic this team once had was totally spent.

Had the leadership team or anyone at the organization sat down and actually worked out, on paper, what they could control vs. what they couldn't, time and effort might've been spent in a more productive direction. In fact, might've been spent in a direction that really *did* win over prospects and therefore created the conditions within which salespeople could've succeeded.

This of course never happened.

What did happen was that one by one, each person on the team came to the same conclusion: I can't make a difference here and I can't succeed. So, everyone quit.

But why did they join the company in the first place? Pretty simple: it was a job with a team that *had* succeeded, it was a job with a team that *believed* it could succeed, and it was a job. Read nearly any book on sales produced in the last 20 years and a silent, subtle through line will become apparent to you: Believe you'll succeed and you'll succeed.

Some books spell it out directly, such as The Power of Positive Thinking, or The Secret (holy shit, this one *eyeroll*), some less directly, such as nearly anything Brian Tracy writes. Belief is pretty good, thinking positively is pretty good, but there's no real "critical" component to it. This is why the whole sales team basically ragequit that SaaS company within two years of excitedly joining it.

If positive thinking is part of the problem, the opposite can't be negative thinking, right? That's true, which is why I'm not advocating it. Instead, what I'm advocating is a more radical departure from both of those unhelpful poles: clear-headed, realistic, slightly-pessimistic, resigned thinking.

Instead of "We're going to take over the world with this product, and I'm going to sell everyone on it," or "This product blows, nobody is going to want to buy it," I'm advocating thinking like this: "This product does some valuable things for some people who use it, I'm going to try my best to find others who want it, and maybe some of them will, but maybe some won't, anyway I'm going to work hard to do it."

Does that statement fill you with excitement? It shouldn't.

What I'm advocating is an attitude, a way of thinking, that replaces passion with consistency.

In a world that's constantly making you feel responsible for everything that happens around you, and wants you to believe you can change the world, the most radical thing you can do is simply recognize how little control you really *do* have. I'm not talking about throwing your hands up and believing you can't control anything. Instead, recognize what you *can't* control and focus only on what you *can*.

The most useful arena to this kind of thinking is sales. Sales is a world *dependent* upon the decisions of others. You can't *make* your prospects do anything. You can't make them choose anything. Another way it's been said is "People hate getting sold but love to buy." The fundamental problem many salespeople have is believing they can get people to buy. They can't, nobody can. People either buy or they don't.

What this book presents instead of unbridled optimism or unlimited self-belief, is a handful of selected passages from the realm of stoic philosophy that are particularly relevant to the chaotic world of sales. They're sober, sometimes pessimistic, and sometimes nearly boring. But they are *relevant*. They're ancient words written by people who knew what living in chaos, dependent entirely on the whims of others, was like.

Epictetus was a slave who earned his freedom and started a school teaching stoicism. Seneca was a politician exiled by people he believed were his colleagues and friends. Marcus Aurelius was emperor of all the Roman Empire at the height of its power, surrounded by yes-men and fighting nearly constant border wars.

From day-to-day, each of these men had to fight battles with chaos. They had to find an inner peace in a world that tried to constantly agitate them. It was necessary for each of these men to perform each and every day. None of them had the luxury of being able to despair, or run away from their problems. All of them needed to find a way to continue. Yet, at the same time, none of them had the convenience of positive thinking. Epictetus knew the harsh realities of slavery, and was aware that a twist of fate could easily land him back in chains. Seneca's life was spared from death simply on a whim from the emperor he served, and had no idea when or if he'd ever be allowed back from exile. Marcus Aurelius couldn't be positive, knowing that hubris from emperors and generals in the past had led to every military loss Rome experienced.

For these men, as many in the ancient world, death was only an arm's length away. The stakes were high, yet they needed to make choices and take action every day. The words they've written have stood the test of time, and come down to us thousands of years later as wisdom we can use in our daily lives. Hell, in our sales jobs; in any job.

From 2,000 years to today, these are lessons meant to make you more effective, more stable, more consistent, and honestly happier. Stoicism was created in a world full of chaos and uncertainty, and bears a strange, uncanny resemblance to the world we walk through every day. They've helped me succeed and achieve a grounded, stable & consistent mindset. They've helped me become the most successful salesperson on more than one team, and then be promoted to lead those teams. They'll do the same for you.

Why do people buy?

So, why does anyone do anything? It's not been a philosophical question I've ever openly debated in a college classroom, but maybe it should be. I've yet to pick up a book on sales and have anyone explain in plain English why anybody buys something. Most of the time books like to pontificate endlessly on how to sell someone on something, and how to win over a prospect, his bosses, his receptionist, and then push for all kinds of up-sells, as if the world of sales is filled only with car dealerships.

People all day long sell themselves on things that no salesperson has ever spoken to them about. Probably all salespeople will be replaced by AI driven human avatars in the cloud in the next decade (probably, some of you will be selling the robots that will soon replace you). But until that techno-apocalypse happens, it's still up to humans to help shepherd someone from not buying into buying. But if people sell themselves, where does wanting to buy come from? And if salespeople are incidental to the sale, why do they exist?

It's my belief that people buy when they see a solution that they trust will help them get what they want, and the reward they'll get is worth more than the money they're paying for the solution.

So the critical factors here are prospect perception, trust, desire for reward, and cost. Someone deciding to buy comes from a balance of all four elements.

When someone tries to convince another person to buy, they're "selling" that other person. Normally, they're playing with one of these four elements. Most critically, the salesperson can control only one element: cost. This is why so many novice salespeople drop cost so quickly. However, salespeople attempt to manipulate all four elements in different ways.

Prospect perception is typically addressed by selling features. "Hey look what it can do!" Is the message of feature selling. The idea is that if the prospect wants a solution, then showing them what the product does will confirm to them that indeed, this product will solve their problem and help them get the reward they want. This is why so many salespeople go to features selling first. Not only does feature selling sell to prospect perception of the solution, but it also has the potential to enhance prospect desire for reward *and* trust that the product will help the prospect gain the reward they seek. However, features selling almost never achieves this.

Instead, salespeople attempt to sell features before the prospect really trusts the *salesperson*. Especially in a complex sales environment, which in our modern world we more and more find ourselves in, prospects tend not to feel heard or understood by the salespeople they deal with, and therefore don't have a lot of trust in any solution the salesperson presents. I can attest that I, unfortunately, often get on a GoToMeeting to watch a salesperson tell me how great their solution is to a problem I don't really have. Many, *many* people, especially in a B2B sales environment, have wasted a ton of time doing this.

So, it's no surprise that there's a tidal wave of literature talking about how to sell yourself as a person first. If the prospect doesn't trust you, then why would they trust your solution and buy anything from you? This makes sense, I guess. This has led to a whole lot of salespeople talking about themselves and why they've come to the conclusion that the product or service they're selling is so overwhelmingly good, they had to join the company and help evangelize it. Pretty cool, I guess.

Despite my slightly derisive attitude, I actually think this *is* the best method to approach sales from, more or less. As you might guess, I mostly think it's done poorly by most salespeople. Let me explain why I think it's the best approach by pulling us back to ancient thought.

Aristotle, student of Plato, who was himself student of Socrates, perhaps the founder of "western thought," wrote a book he called Rhetoric. In it, he attempted to catalogue all the ways of arguing and winning and argument. Although sales isn't really an argument, it's pretty similar. If someone already saw your solution as *the solution* they'd just buy it. So, somewhere in their brain they need some convincing.

In the book, the old man breaks down the three things you need to win over someone: ethos, pathos, and logos. Ethos is where we get the word "ethics" from, and basically translates to "character" in English. Pathos is where we get the words "pathetic" and "pathological" from. In English, "pathos" translates to "emotion." Finally "logos" is where we get the word "logic" from and translates to "the word" in English. It's best to think of logos as "reasons" why someone would do something; this is where you provide data, etc.

Think about having all three in sales like this: If prospects trust you and trust your product, that's ethos. If prospects believe testimonials and see your product in action and excitedly believe that your product will solve their problem, that's pathos. If prospects see the data and know that the ROI on a purchase from you is in their favor, that's logos. If you have all three, nobody but a total idiot wouldn't buy. Everyone would buy.

Lots of startup literature talks about logos by making sure you have a solution that really works. Peter Thiel's famous "10x better" is a good example. If your product is 10x better in some aspect than all competitors, there's no reason in the world not to use it. Meanwhile, lots of sales literature addresses pathos by talking about "building a vision" and "using good customer stories." Lots of sales literature talks about prospects "buying from emotion." This is true, but it's not the only reason prospects buy. When it comes to big ticket items, savvy prospects try to take emotion out of the equation as much as possible; that's why many firms employ procurement people. Procurement people are born with a special gene that prevents them from having any *real* emotions the way a normal human person has them. Am I joking?

The trend in sales writing lately is to finally come back around to ethos. It was Aristotle's belief that the character of the speaker *did* have a meaningful impact on the message. I think we all know in our gut this is true. The character of the speaker being integral to the message is why the George W. Bush administration had Colin Powell address the UN Security Council about Iraq, and not Dick Cheney. The speaker makes a difference. Lots of sales writing lately has talked about how to be someone that other people want to buy from. Honestly, this is super useful.

"How can I become the kind of person that prospects want to buy from," is a more productive question to answer than "How can I sell more prospects." They sound similar, they're aiming at providing the same outcome, but their answers look profoundly different.

In a way, your sales efforts are attempting to answer *some* question above the others. You might as well make which question you're trying to answer explicit and know what it is. I used to say to my sales team every day "How can we be the kind of salespeople that prospects are *excited* to get a phone call from?" Now, there either *is* or *is not* an answer to that question. It's a metaphysical question. If there is, then the goal is to find it. If there isn't, then the pursuit of it doesn't matter. But if there isn't an answer to the question, then I don't know what the hell the point of doing any sales is. I guess that's my Pascal's Wager (nobody reading this book thought it would be full of this many philosophy references).

Once we've decided our leading question, we're in a better position to answer other questions. What tools and resources would the kind of salesperson people want to buy from have? Easy, he or she would have great case studies and customer stories that answered questions and would present them in an easy-to-understand manner that prospects could relate to. Bang.

If people buy because they perceive a solution that they trust will help deliver the reward they want for a price they're willing to pay, then you just have to be the kind of salesperson who embodies characteristics of trustworthiness, adding value, and authentic interest in your prospect's satisfaction. This isn't impossible, it's just challenging. It's difficult because the perception of being trustworthy, of being a value-add, of being authentic isn't up to you; it's up to your prospects. They choose to place trust, or believe your authenticity, or see what you do as valuable. You don't have control over that.

This is why stoicism is so important to sales; you can only choose what you can do, and the prospect has to pick up where you leave off.

Prospects tend to buy because they can't do something on their own. They buy because there's an asymmetrical relationship between them and the product or service they're considering. The product or service is more valuable than their money. These decisions are based on their beliefs and their feelings. The perception that what they're paying for is going to do what they hope it does is founded on trust. Trust is the consistency of action over time. Therefore consistency is extremely important in sales, and from salespeople.

Stoicism will help you keep an even keel. While staying steady, people will trust you. When they trust you, they'll believe you. When they believe you, they'll buy from you. Sales is about relationships, and being the kind of person that people want to buy from means being a valuable person in a prospect's life; and that means starting with being a valuable person in your own life. Be good to yourself. Stay steady, and you'll be steady in your prospect's life.

There's a theory that I tend to agree with that people only buy from salespeople they see as higher status than themselves. The idea is that only people who are perceived to have more value and status can convey value; everyone else would only take it. I think this theory stands to reason. The fact that studies show that taller people tend to earn more as salespeople, except in a remote sales position, helps support this theory (fact check me, dear reader).

There's a second theory about human behavior this first one combines with too, which states that people who react tend to be perceived as less valuable. I think this also makes sense; if you're powerful, then things don't bother you, because you'll just be fine. If you're constantly swinging from mood to mood depending on what's going around you then you QED aren't steady or stable. It's important to also note that whenever two parties are engaged in a contest, or in a game, the one who's *reacting* tends to be the lower-status and losing party. The Navy SEALs openly talk about trying to keep their opponent constantly reacting to *them*, rather than having time to put a plan together. Powerful people are *on task*, low-status people are *reactive*.

This is important because stoicism is a good bulwark against being reactive, against both being, and being perceived as low status. Even if you have a good product or service but you're reactive, thrown by prospects, and carried away by your thoughts and feelings, nobody is going to want to buy anything from you. Your pitch isn't going to reassure anyone. No prospect wants to sit in a GoToMeeting and think "Man, this guy *really* needs me to buy from him."

Being a good stoic in your sales job will fulfill Aristotle's three core tenets of rhetoric and, if you have a product that does actually help deliver the reward a prospect is looking for, you'll make sales left and right. Not only will you make sales, but you'll have a great life being steady. Not only will you be steady, but you'll be joyous, because nothing will throw you. You'll be a sage.

People will buy because they will trust you, believe when you say their product will help them gain the reward they want, and because buying makes more sense than not buying. As a sage, as a stoic, you'll coolly help them see this by being the kind of person that others want to buy from. That's why people will buy.

A Quick Note About The Text

The quotes for the following sections are available online. One of the best things about studying stoicism is how accessible it is. You can find many of the original texts online in their entirety, so you don't even have to buy.

All material presented in this book is licensed under a Creative Commons Attribution-ShareAlike 3.0 United States License.

Here are the links for where to find the original texts cited in this book:

Epictetus
    The Enchiridion: http://www.perseus.tufts.edu/hopper/text?doc=Perseus:text:1999.01.0237:text=enc

Seneca
    Moral Letters to Lucilius: https://en.wikisource.org/wiki/Moral_letters_to_Lucilius
    De Brevitate Vitae: https://en.wikisource.org/wiki/On_the_shortness_of_life

Marcus Aurelius
    Meditations: http://classics.mit.edu/Antoninus/meditations.html

PART TWO
EPICTETUS

A Slave to His Job

For me, picking up a copy of Epictetus' teaching was like a throwing a cold water onto a man on fire. For someone with a mind that won't stop turning over anxieties, difficulties, scenarios, in short, ruminations, his words were a kind of antidote.

"But what if!?" My brain would scream at me. It was like this for years, since I was a kid. Having a mother that worried about thing after thing after thing didn't help, but even having the calmest mother wouldn't have helped. The world itself wants to assault your mind with constant concerns. Is the train going to be on time? What happens if I miss my flight? Where will the money for retirement come from? All these questions circulate like a kind of hurricane of the mind; unchecked they blow throughout one's brain and do all kinds of damage to one's sense of self, plans, and personality.

I wish I'd discovered this guy when I was a teenager, it would've been perfect.

Why? Because when you're a teenager, nothing in your life is up to you - almost all of your time is spoken for. You go to school, you maybe work, you do homework, maybe you do some kind of athletics. Mostly, all the adults you grew up around tell you what to do. You feel like a prisoner, or a slave. And this was exactly what Epictetus was for most of his life.

Epictetus was born in 55 A.D. in Phrygia, a province of the Roman Empire. No one knows his birth name; the name "Epictetus" is a derivative of the Greek word *epiktetos*, which means "gained" or "acquired." He acquired everything he had in his life. When he was a child he was taken to Rome, where he lived as a slave.

In Rome, Epictetus worked in a position with a wealthy public man and eventually was granted his freedom as a teenager. In his late 30's, the Roman Emperor Domitian famously banished all philosophers from the city of Rome. Too many questions being asked apparently. Just like the other stoics that inform this book, a rough life of stress, uncertainty, and ultimately banishment characterized Epictetus' time.

By the time he was kicked out of Rome though, he had acquired enough knowledge to found a school; which was kind of the ancient world's equivalent of being a life coach. He moved to Greece and there instructed many, many people including the famous ancient historian Arrian (yes, even the ancient world had historians), and even the emperor Hadrian (who famously proclaimed "We're going to build a wall and get the Picts to pay for it!" <— This isn't true, but it's funny to think about).

At every turn, Epictetus' life is a kind of beautiful argument for the idea that anyone can really do anything. Lamed as a child so he couldn't run away from being a slave, eventually the most powerful man in the known world, Hadrian, listened to what he had to say. Even today, more than just your humble narrator has been influenced by him. His modern pupils include guys like Vietnam pilot James Stockdale, who relied on Epictetus when he was shot down behind enemy lines.

He famously gained a reputation for being kind of a jerk to his students, as a tool for forcing them to get a thick skin, which is *sort of* what Stoicism is about. His student, Arrian, transcribed all kinds of mean and sarcastic things he'd say to his students. If the reader decides they want to indulge in the ancient world's version of insult comedy, take a look at Epictetus' *Discourses*, they're a laugh riot.

Much like many ancient philosophers who pontificated wisdom almost haphazardly, he was too lazy to write anything down. Epictetus has bequeathed to us nothing of his own accord, but Arrian, just like Plato before him, wrote the words of his master down and boy, they're pretty good. So, either because he was so brilliant that he inspired someone to copy his diatribes down, or because Arrian's the real genius, it doesn't matter, we have his great wisdom to read today.

What follows is a series of selected passages from one of the most influential books not only in my life, but in all of stoic philosophy. Like I said, when I discovered this tiny handbook it was like a revitalizing drink of water that cooled my worries. I had to tell everyone about it. Anyone who'd listen would hear incessantly about the basic tenets of stoic philosophy. I stopped getting invitations for drinks, but it didn't matter, because I couldn't control whether or not I got invited to something anyway!

My little handbook by Epictetus went everywhere with me. In fact, "handbook" is a pretty good name because that's exactly what it's called in Greek; "Enchiridion" translates exactly to "handbook." As it applies to sales, its first few tenets are the core 20% that makes the 80% of sales possible. Read it, live it. I encourage the reader to reread these passages daily and keep them at hand for tense or difficult moments. I always found that a quick read over Epictetus relieved my mind of worries.

THE ENCHIRIDION TENET 1

There are things which are within our power, and there are things which are beyond our power. Within our power are opinion, aim, desire, aversion, and, in one word, whatever affairs are our own. Beyond our power are body, property, reputation, office, and, in one word, whatever are not properly our own affairs.

Now, the things within our power are by nature free, unrestricted, unhindered; but those beyond our power are weak, dependent, restricted, alien. Remember, then, that if you attribute freedom to things by nature dependent, and take what belongs to others for your own, you will be hindered, you will lament, you will be disturbed, you will find fault both with gods and men. But if you take for your own only that which is your own, and view what belongs to others just as it really is, then no one will ever compel you, no one will restrict you, you will find fault with no one, you will accuse no one, you will do nothing against your will; no one will hurt you, you will not have an enemy, nor will you suffer any harm.

Aiming therefore at such great things, remember that you must not allow yourself any inclination, however slight, towards the attainment of the others; but that you must entirely quit some of them, and for the present postpone the rest. But if you would have these, and possess power and wealth likewise, you may miss the latter in seeking the former; and you will certainly fail of that by which alone happiness and freedom are procured.

Seek at once, therefore, to be able to say to every unpleasing semblance, " You are but a semblance and by no means the real thing." And then examine it by those rules which you have; and first and chiefly, by this: whether it concerns the things which are within our own power, or those which are not; and if it concerns anything beyond our power, be prepared to say that it is nothing to you.

Focus on your locus of control

Reading this passage was like a punch in the face to me. I've always been the kid who needed to almost get hit by a car in order to know to not cross the street. I needed to have it spelled out, as simply as possible, by a guy two millennia ago to actually get it: DO NOT WORRY ABOUT THINGS YOU CAN'T CONTROL!

This is perhaps the foundational, bedrock belief of Stoicism: You can't control what you can't control, so let it go. If you try and build a life around the things you don't have control over, the whims of others, what the future will be, you're going to be unhappy and pissed off all the time. Don't do that. Instead, with everything in your life you should be asking "Is this within my power or not?"

In sales, you job is *necessarily* about the things beyond your power. Is it in within your power to get a prospect to answer the phone? Is it within your power to get the CEO of another company to sign on the dotted line? Is it within your power to make your numbers this year?

Actually, it isn't within *your* power to do any of these things. It never was, and it never will be.

Probably, a lot of you salespeople will be reading this and saying things like "It IS within MY power! I have the power to make my number." No you don't. Don't be dense.

This is actually one of the biggest lessons Stoicism has to offer: be very careful about what *you can do* and then focus on that. If you can't control making your number for the year, what *can* you focus on? Instead of being worried about the number, focus instead on the activities you know are within your power to control. Know your pitch, study your prospects, increase the number of cold calls, write sharper cold emails; these activities *do* lie within your power, and are much more solid ground for building on.

Often, when considering what is and is not in my control, once I'm realistic and remove from what's outside of my control from my thoughts, I'm left with more options that I can focus on. The thought exercise "How could I hit my number in the last three months of this year if I focus only on what I *do* have control over?" Is useful. Working on a whiteboard one evening in the office I came up with this:

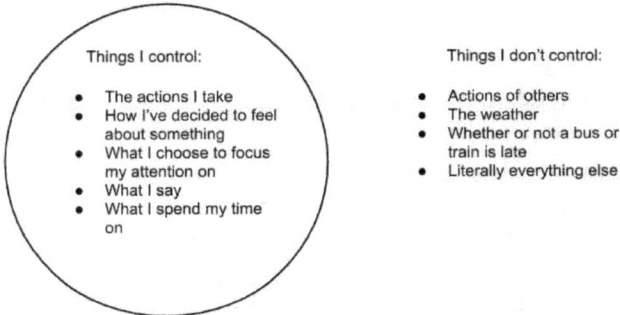

Things I control:

- The actions I take
- How I've decided to feel about something
- What I choose to focus my attention on
- What I say
- What I spend my time on

Things I don't control:

- Actions of others
- The weather
- Whether or not a bus or train is late
- Literally everything else

Okay, maybe not *that* helpful to sales yet, but focusing in on what *I could do* in the last three months, I came up with this:

```
            Things I can do/control:                    Things I can't do/control:

      •  Making good offers - matching price
         points prospect's have said they'd buy at      •  Whether or not someone
      •  Connect with more people in prospect's            will buy
         organization, bring them into the              •  Whether or not someone
         conversation                                      will reply
      •  Research & message 10 more new                  •  Hitting my number
         prospects every morning before 9am with
         targeted cold messages
      •  Sending tighter outreach based on my
         research and relationships with prospects
         for an extra hour at the end of every day
      •  Rehearsing and memorizing my pitches
         and talk tracks
      •  Studying our competition and our best
         strategies & selling points against them
```

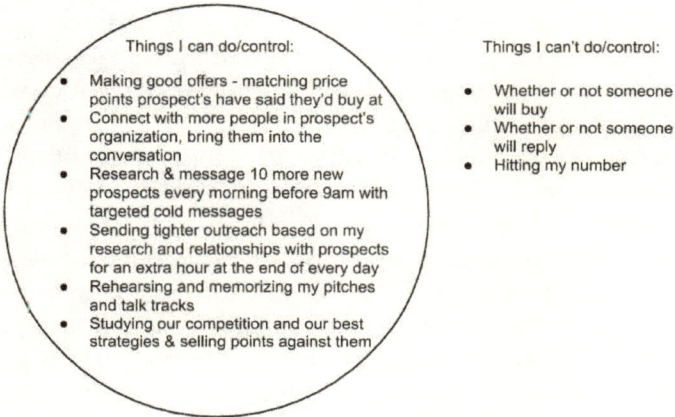

Once I've removed from the table things I can't control, my mind is able to focus more on *what I can do*. Spending an extra hour a day just messaging prospects with offers to move forward, connecting with more people who would be decision makers in their organizations, and researching competitors they might be using and the most convincing arguments to switch, is a solid strategy that *you do* control. This is exactly what I did in the fall of 2015, and ended up blowing away my number by January first.

By moving the focus off of what you cannot control, mainly, the decision of others, and instead focus on what you can do, new options open. Maybe email two people at an organization at once, send an invite to a five minute meeting to pitch your best offer ever, put together a purchase agreement and just send it over to your prospect for signing (or their CEO). Do these sound a bit aggressive? Maybe, but they are actions you can take. After you've made some decisions on what you can do, practice the art of stoic resignation, as Epictetus mentions above. Taking actions that aim to achieve your goal, once you've thrown the spear, you can't control it in flight nor how it will land. Take the best actions you can, focus on what you can do, and then practice resignation and let go of whether or not someone will respond to you.

Beyond the simple call for letting go what you can't control, there's a deeper message I take from this passage: "Be steady, forget and ignore things that make you unsteady." We might call this "Stoic steadiness." What is it? It's simple, it's not allowing your impressions, your feelings, to upset you. Your aim is your goal, and your path is whatever you've taken, and now the way you're walking it is steady.

This is an important lesson for everyone in business, but especially in sales. If Zig Ziglar is right, and sales is about a transfer of emotions, then it *absolutely necessary* for the salesperson to be *the most confident and steady* person in the sales conversation. If a salesperson is upset, capsized, overwhelmed, nobody is going to buy.

How do we exercise steadiness? By practicing recognizing what we can't control and letting go of it while moving toward our goals.

Maybe you're a salesperson at a startup, maybe you're a salesperson at a large corporation, maybe you're not a salesperson, and in that case, thank you mom for reading my new book. Whatever you do, if you're in an organization that's struggling to hit numbers and grow, the pattern is very similar: Someone calls a meeting, and at that meeting the CEO or whatever other ranking executive that's in the room begins asking a bunch of pointed questions about different initiatives in the business. "What about trying to prospect into restaurants? What about pitching our new product? What's happening with our content marketing? What about following up with old prospects? How's outreach for those upcoming conferences and events coming?" Que everyone's blood pressure spiking.

"We can't do everything," is a phrase I say to a lot of CEO's at companies I consult for. For some reason, in todays modern world of business, the predominant executive feeling is that everyone should be doing everything all at once. This is how you drown.

Instead, focus on only what you can control, in a simple, straightforward way. Make reasonable progress toward that goal at a steady, deliberate pace. Although it isn't Stoicism, remember the message from the ancient parable: it was the turtle that first finished the race, not the hare.

THE ENCHIRIDION TENET 2

Remember that desire demands the attainment of that of which you are desirous; and aversion demands the avoidance of that to which you are averse; that he who fails of the object of his desires is disappointed; and he who incurs the object of his aversion is wretched. If, then, you shun only those undesirable things which you can control, you will never incur anything which you shun; but if you shun sickness, or death, or poverty, you will run the risk of wretchedness. Remove [the habit of] aversion, then, from all things that are not within our power, and apply it to things undesirable, which are within our power. But for the present altogether restrain desire; for if you desire any of the things not within our own power, you must necessarily be disappointed; and you are not yet secure of those which are within our power, and so are legitimate objects of desire. Where it is practically necessary for you to pursue or avoid anything, do even this with discretion, and gentleness, and moderation.

———————————————————

Okay, so if the world is full of two things, things in our power and things aren't, now the question is, what do we want to do? I really beat the horse of where to spend your time and focus to death in the last diatribe (and so did Epictetus), so let's move on and look now to how to imagine our desires. Basically, Epictetus is saying that there are two other distinctions we make: things we want, and things we don't want. Pretty simple. After this, we are averse to, and move away from things we don't want, and move toward things we do want or desire.

The *real* problem in life comes from attempting to get *or avoid* things that you want which are outside your power to control, you're going to be disappointed (not getting things you desire) or wretched (getting things you want to avoid). The examples Epictetus uses for things people don't want are always extreme, like death, poverty, sickness, etc. But they need not be this serious; quite frankly, they can be small. Did you want a donut on your way to the office, but the donut stand you normally visit is closed today? You're going to be disappointed. Did you want to avoid being late for a meeting, but you got stopped by a train that broke down as it crossed the tracks in front of you? You're going to be wretched.

Wait? Isn't this kind of saying the same thing the last one said? Eh, kinda. You shouldn't get mad at Stoics for repeating the same thing all the time; doctors have been talking about the dangers of red meat for decades, and the same three chords are in every pop song. Clearly, reminding people for thousands of years to calm down about the stuff they can't control still hasn't totally worked; that's why I've *also* written a book about it.

Once I worked with a guy at a restaurant. He wasn't the luckiest guy. In fact, he mostly saw his life as "wretched." This guy worked in the kitchen at the restaurant and was a real Negative Nancy. He complained every day about how unlucky or bad things would befall him in life. "They're probably going to send another dish of mine back tonight," he'd say. Then, when this inevitably did happen, he'd curse himself, he'd curse life, and then would get all bent out of shape for hours. He lived in a tiny apartment he was always behind in rent on, and apparently, according to whatever friends he did have, he hadn't been laid in over a year. I felt bad for him. But really, truly, the major fear of his was getting fired. While out smoking behind the restaurant he'd complain "Oh man, my days are numbered, I'm always getting fired from a job, I'm sure this guy is going to can me sometime soon." Every day it went on like this until, lo and behold, one day he got fired.

"I freaking KNEW IT!" he yelled as he threw off his apron and left the kitchen. Later that day we caught up with him at the local watering hole for restaurant industry types. He had gotten drunk and was still complaining. "These things always happen to me," he muttered over and over.

I felt bad for him, I still feel bad for him. For his sake I hope he's turned it around. But notice, as Epictetus did 2,000 years ago: at no point did *he take actions within his control*. What this guy and the failing, wretched salesman have in common is the inability to notice and focus on *what they can control*. He couldn't control whether or not he was going to get fired, that decision wasn't up to him, but he *could* control things like knowing the recipes, knowing how to cook them properly and on time, and his attitude toward the job. Instead, he *desired the wrong things*, and desired to be employed. If he had desired to be a good cook, he never would've had to worry about being fired. No restaurant owner in his right mind would fire a good cook, and even if he did, that cook would soon find offers from other places to work.

The calling is to something deeper, something that employment is *built* on. The calling is to cook good food, not to be a cook.

Years ago, when I was still a Sales Development Rep at a marketing technology company, I worked with a sales guy who was basically the same as the cook I worked with back at the restaurant. He wasn't *quite* as wretched, but he was close. Time and time again he'd hear back from prospects he'd had "a great conversation" with, only to discover that, weeks later, they'd decided to work with someone else. "What is with these prospects!?" he'd sometimes say exasperatedly when talking about this. "It's like, c'mon!" Yeah, come on and work with someone else. Similarly, later at a pub, after a few beers, he'd start lamenting the situation. "I just don't get it, all these deals dematerialize in front of me. It's like none of these guys want to buy!" Yeah, none of them want to buy *from you*.

It was exactly the same - instead of trying to avoid what was in his power to avoid, spending too long getting back to prospects, connecting with and building rapport with multiple members of their team, asking really good questions, adding value to all of their initiatives, he spent time worried about whether or not the prospect was going to buy. So, it shouldn't have been a surprise when they went with someone else.

Once again, the deeper calling isn't to close deals, technically that's up to someone else, the calling is to *sell*. Selling is the term used to wrap up a whole bunch of activities under one word. Selling is connecting, is listening, is asking good questions, is trying to understand what someone else wants to do and then adding value to that. If you happen to have a product or service that assists someone with their goal, then they can buy it.

Where do sales come from? Why does someone buy? What makes someone make the decision to go with one company rather than another? For me, it's trust. In fact, I created an equation about trust:

* * *

$$\text{Trust} = \frac{\text{Consistency of Action}}{\text{Time}}$$

People trust what they know, and what they know increases with exposure. Taking action in a consistent manner, over time, leads to trust from a prospect. If people trust YOU, then they can trust what you say. When you say "I really think buying from us will work well for you, and this is our best deal," they'll trust it. In other words, trust comes from having *a relationship* with someone.

Relationships are based on an exchange of value. Friends exchange good times. Business partners exchange money. You can only control *your* side of the relationship, and the Enchiridion's second tenet speaks directly to this. Someone who wants to be in a relationship can only control their actions. If all exchange in business is based on relationships then the best thing to do is focus on what you can do on your side of that relationship, and build trust.

Reflect on how you would like to be treated if you were a prospect, reflect on what value your product or service really does offer, and to whom, and now enter the marketplace with that perspective in hand. Talk to people in the way you'd want them to talk to you; that's what you have control over.

Apply aversion to "I don't want to miss my number this month" isn't helpful. It's more helpful to apply aversion to "I don't want to get to 6pm and realize I haven't made any cold calls." It's *more* helpful to apply attainment to "I want to get 30 cold calls done by 10am." Taking actions to attain something you *want* is tantamount to taking actions to avoid something you *don't*.

Lets imagine then, that the end of the month comes, and you don't make your number. However, you've been thinking and working like a Stoic all month. You look back, from the position of the 31st and realize that all Monday through Friday workdays you maximized your time, you worked diligently and made the cold calls you imaged would capture your goal every day. You practiced your pitch and knew your talk tracks. In fact, you *did* get meetings, move deal conversations forward, and looked like you were on track to hit your number, but you didn't, and you can't quite figure out why.

In this scenario, what's the problem? While it's *true* that the "problem" is that you didn't hit your number, by all outward appearances you did everything you could do to attain that goal. If you're a Stoic about it, and benchmarking your internal well-being only with things you *can control*, then you should feel no real disappointment. Not only should you feel no real disappointment (aside from perhaps the very light feeling that you did want something and it didn't happen), but you should feel comfortable defending your effort to others and to yourself.

Now, there's many a salesperson reading this and thinking "If I worked as hard as you said I did, and I didn't make my number, others would think I should feel ashamed for not achieving it, if I *did* really work that hard." This is foolish thinking. Breaking it down, this thought is trying to determine what one's feelings *should be* based on how *others* perceive the situation. You might just as well try and build a house during a windstorm. The question is how do *you* judge your effort and achievement? You are ultimately the one you must answer to at the end of the day, and at the end of your life.

I used to be someone who constantly thought in terms of what others believed, thought, or perceived about me. On the Myers-Briggs personality test, I'm an ENFP type, and apparently this is endemic to us. If you don't know that that means, Myers-Briggs is about one rung above astrology in terms of predicting anything about you. Basically, it means I absorb everyone's thoughts and opinions around me. Probably if I live to be 100 I'm going to end up still having to be careful about basing my sense of self on the perceptions of others. When I read The Enchiridion's second tenet though, something in me shifted. "If I base my well-being on avoiding being disliked, I'm going to release control of myself to the whims of others." Whether or not you feel you did a good job is up to you, not up to others.

In the ancient world, people had more appreciation for the mysterious whims of the gods. Whoever those gods were, they had all kinds of different desires that were completely opaque to humans. Zeus could summon lightning to strike on a wedding day, Hera could transform into a snake and eat a child, Poseidon could summon a wave to wipe away an entire town (what a jerk). Who knows why any of them did anything? In the modern, humanistic world we now live in, we sometimes expect that each person should have complete command of their life and everything that happens to them. This is complete madness. The world is complete chaos. There's almost no order to anything. The fact that *anything* works out should be celebrated, because it was probably on accident.

"So how could I work so hard and miss my number?" You're probably still noodling on from a few paragraphs ago. Good question. If you're an experienced salesperson you probably understand it already. Here's how:

In the fall of 2015 I connected with someone at a very large children's retail brand. If you live in the USA, and you have a baby, you've probably bought stuff from them. At the time I was working at a major mobile marketing company in Chicago. They did great work, and this brand could've used the service my firm provided. The conversation took a long time to develop, but over time they became more and more interested and finally were hooked. It took about nine months. In the summer of 2016, they were ready to pull the trigger. It was a *huge* deal, starting at about the seven-figure mark, and likely increasing toward the eight-figure mark. In the final stages of the RFP process (a long, annoying, frustrating procurement process that large organizations use to figure out who they're going to choose as a partner - kind of like The Bachelor). Everyone was biting their nails, this was going to really put a dent over our sales team's number and pull us over the line.

Finally, we got the call... we had been accepted as the preferred partner! Our team freaked out, it was great news. We flew into contracting and sent over the documents. This was going to make my year, going to fill my wallet with some fat cash and a huge bonus. Everyone shook hands, our contacts at the prospect's organization were excited and ready to get to work with us. There was only one thing left to do, and that was sign on the dotted line. We sent over the contract, they printed it out, and they left it on the CMO's desk to sign just after his morning meeting.

Then the CMO was fired in that meeting.

We got the news. Nobody believed it was real. It felt like falling off a cliff. For days I racked my brain trying to think what I could've done differently. How could I have accounted for the CMO leaving? Why couldn't I hit my number? What would a better salesperson have done to get around this? Could I even trust myself? I was in such turmoil about it that I picked my copy of The Enchiridion back up and started reading.

"Oh that's right," I remembered. "Shit just happens sometimes and there's nothing you can do about it."

That company eventually replaced the CMO, and my initial suspicions about our value prop being good for them were also correct; they signed with us. It took another 18 months, but the new CMO was won over, they went through a second RFP process, and they determined, once again, that this was the best course of action for them. I eventually got the bonus. From then on, I never had any expectations with deals. "Things will either work out or they won't," I'd say to myself. Does it sound depressing? Maybe, based on your perspective. But for me it sounds realistic. I'll never waste any time or energy or focus beating myself up, just focusing on my work and getting things done to move forward.

Just as Epictetus says "Where it is practically necessary for you to pursue or avoid anything, do even this with discretion, and gentleness, and moderation."

THE ENCHIRIDION TENET 3

With regard to whatever objects either delight the mind, or contribute to use, or are tenderly beloved, remind yourself of what nature they are, beginning with the merest trifles: if you have a favorite cup, that it is but a cup of which you are fond, - for thus, if it is broken, you can bear it; if you embrace your child, or your wife, that you embrace a mortal, - and thus, if either of them dies, you can bear it.

Yeeeeeesh - Here's where the Stoic school really gets its dour reputation from. "Hey, do you love someone? Yeah, remind yourself that they're gonna be dead and you could lose them!" These guys must've had a ton of friends.

In 2008 I had the opportunity to work at the US Embassy in Paris. It. Was. AMAZING! For the whole summer I worked in downtown Paris. I ate croissants and drank wine by the Seine with a bunch of other expats I met. I dated a French woman. She was just as beautiful as the city. This was the summer George W. Bush came out on his European tour and I got to be on his luggage reception team. I handled the mountain bike he took everywhere with him and when I dropped it off at where he was staying, the US Ambassador's residence, I met the guy. Truly, I'd never liked him, but in that moment, he was so friendly and so disarming, that I found myself grinning from ear-to-ear. It might've been the best summer of my life. On my last day of my internship, the team I was working with bought a coffee mug for me. "US Embassy - Paris" it said on it along with the seal of the United States. It was the thing I loved the most. Every time I looked at it I remembered that whole summer, friends, adventures, fun, excitement,

Paris.

My mother broke it three weeks after getting home.

So it goes.

I'm sure you get it, but, to spell it out, for me, this one means recognizing the impermanence of things. Literally, I had a cup that I was fond of, and it broke.

You love your deals? Your prospects? Your position as top salesperson? Get ready, because all that stuff is going to go away. Deals fall apart. Prospects turn on you (prospects and girlfriends, the most disloyal people around). This is the world we're in. They say to be great at something you have to kill your darlings, well, you might as well, because your darlings are going to be dead anyway.

Two lessons in and you're probably already like "I get it, I can't control things so I shouldn't have feelings about it." Well, get ready, because I'm going to pound that lesson home in every chapter, homie.

Beyond just recognizing that there are things outside of your control though, The Enchiridion's third tenet gives us some additional direction about how we should be planning our lives, given that so little is up to you.

Firstly, remind yourself that things can, and will fall apart, at some point. Everything you have is impermanent. Some people think that this is a really disappointing, tragic way of looking at the world. Maybe. But also, it's maybe a much, much better way of looking at the world. Instead of living in an illusion that everything around you is going to be the way it is forever, and because of that reason *you can take it for granted*, you instead recognize that *every moment you have is special and won't come again*. Do you like you house or apartment? That's awesome. Please take a moment and feel all the appreciation well up inside you. Do you love your girlfriend or boyfriend and think the she or he is gorgeous? That's so good. Savor it. One day you won't be together, and they won't be beautiful any more.

Don't just do this with things you *like*, though, although that is probably the best use of this exercise. Remind yourself that when things are going badly, that situation is also just as transient as when something is going good. All things pass away, including moments you want to scream and quit and punch something. Once you realize that everything is impermanent, the burden of difficult situations becomes much lighter. Are you frustrated that a prospect seems to be taking up all of your time, or does it seem daunting that you're always working to get something going. Well, buck up, because it'll all be done soon anyway. One way or another, you'll be past it.

The next implication is easier told through a parable. We'll call it, the parable of the sexually frustrated boy.

Okay, so, I wasn't a boy, I was a man. I was a young man. But I was so horny and so sexually frustrated, I was like a living anime character. It was just the case. From my teens into my early 20's I really had trouble with women. Surely, everybody does. My case was acutely bad though; I had had a girlfriend for a few minutes in high school, and everyone wondered why I couldn't get female attention, but I just couldn't. Years went by. All of my friends got partners and one-by-one lost their "V card." Except me.

Day-by-day this would burn on me. I'd go to class, I'd see attractive women. I'd go to work, I'd see attractive women. I'd try to talk to one, and for whatever reason it wouldn't work out. I could never figure out why. For most people, they kind of just figure it out. I didn't. I had no idea what to do. Things got worse, and the prospect of exiting my early 20's still a virgin loomed over me. It was terrifying and frustrating. Big time.

What do you do in a situation like this? You Google. You look up an expert. Or at least, I did. Looking up all the best dating coaches, I eventually listened to an interview with one who I thought made sense. He wasn't a sleazy guy. He didn't advocate "running patterns" or "dating hypnosis" or "cocky-funny" or any other weird jargon or terms. He was just a fun guy and he was actually married to a really fun, cool woman who did a lot of coaching with him. Then I saw he was coming to Chicago, and I jumped at the chance to train with him.

After a day of classroom training with some other students, he pulled me aside. "How come you can't get laid man?" He asked me. "You're a decent looking guy, you're funny, you can talk to people. What's up?" I told him I didn't know. "Alright," he said. "We'll figure it out 'in the field.'" That night he made me approach groups of people in bars. I kept crashing and burning. After one he pulled me aside.

"Dude, I got it," he said. "You're putting too much pressure on yourself. Every time you go into meet people and approach, you want it to work out. It's not going to work out." I was dumbfounded. What the hell was he even saying? I stared at him blankly.

"Okay," I said. He rolled his eyes.

"Look," he said. "You want to *not lose*. You're going in with all the energy in the world of making sure you don't lose. And that's getting you in your head. You want every conversation you have with a woman to work out; you want her to just immediately be attracted to you. That isn't going to happen. It isn't going to happen because you're making it weird in the interaction, but it also isn't going to happen because it just *isn't*.

"Not everyone is for everyone else. Things aren't going to work out. You getting laid isn't about talking to *a woman*, it's about talking to *women*."

At that last line, it landed. It isn't about *a conversation*, it's about *conversations*.

Most of the deals you're going to develop aren't going to work out. If they all did, you'd be literally the best salesperson on the planet. The key is to recognize this and just continue to build more. Open more doors, build more relationships. Within reason, just develop what makes sense. Just like me being an idiot with women for so long, accept that failure is part of the process; things outside of your control will happen and derail your plans. You'll be far more successful if you just let it slide off and move to the next one. Don't take it personally. Keep your head on straight, and like me, eventually you'll find one that wants to get into bed with you.

In sales, in dating, in Stoicism, in life, it isn't about the one thing you're doing, it's about the process and act of doing it. Anything you have is impermanent: your health, your partner, your wealth, your deals-in-pipeline. So focus your efforts on what you can control and forget the rest. Don't spend time expecting results that haven't occurred yet, but spend your focus, time, and energy reasonably pursuing your goals. If fate takes something away from you then so be it. You'll keep right on going and making the best of it.

The number of deals you'll have that won't work out will always outnumber the number of ones that will. In fact, the more you have that won't, probably the more you'll have that will. So don't sweat it. Remember that everything that you have going probably won't work out. Now celebrate when it does.

THE ENCHIRIDION TENET 4

When you set about any action, remind yourself of what nature the action is. If you are going to bathe, represent to yourself the incidents usual in the bath, - some persons pouring out, others pushing in, others scolding, others pilfering. And thus you will more safely go about this action, if you say to yourself, " I will now go to bathe, and keep my own will in harmony with nature." And so with regard to every other action. For thus, if any impediment arises in bathing, you will be able to say, "It was not only to bathe that I desired, but to keep my will in harmony with nature; and I shall not keep it thus, if I am out of humor at things that happen."

For years of my life I never saw a movie I didn't like. It didn't matter what it was. In the 90's and early aughts, I went to the movies with family, friends, and saw good movies, and bad movies. I liked all of them. It didn't matter how much my friends would leave the theater complaining how bad it was, I still enjoyed it.

My track record at liking movies was unflappable. Ghost Rider, Ballistic: Ecks vs. Sever, The Matrix Reloaded, Mortal Kombat: Annihilation, Spawn, Judge Dredd, Batman and Robin, the list of terrible movies ran long and in an act that my friends thought was genuinely trying to get their respective goats, I liked all of them. After the movie, we'd end up at Denny's and would argue about the dumpster fire we just witnessed. My friends would meticulously deconstruct all the frustrating ways the movie ended up short. Funnily enough, and much to their continued anger, I would tend to agree with them.

"How the hell can you like these movies!?" They'd shout.

"I don't know," I'd say back. "I guess they're bad, but, I kind of liked the whole thing. I mean, I just went to go to the movies, get some popcorn, and chill with you guys, not to have my mind blown."

Little did I know I was practicing Epictetus' fourth tenet.

I liked every movie I went to because I always expected most movies to not be that good. I didn't expect them to be bad either, I just didn't expect them to be good. For me, I just liked getting popcorn, watching movie previews, and seeing things happen on screen. When I thought about going to the movies, I imagined riding in the car and joking with my friends, I imagined getting popcorn in the lobby and buying snow caps and flirting with the cute girls behind the counter. I imagined turning to my friends during the movie and making jokes and laughing and didn't really care about the movie at all. So, when I headed to the movies, my expectations were about things I more or less could control, my friends were all focused on what they *couldn't control*.

Whether or not a movie is good isn't up to you, whether or not you have fun *is*.

I've done a lot of strange things in my life. Sometimes when I'm at a dinner party and comparing life stories with others, I don't think it's even a fair fight. I've lived in Paris, done comedy in Iceland, was homeless, helped close multi-million dollar deals, and got in an MMA cage and fought a guy. It's true, I put on gloves, got in a cage, someone hit a bell, and I fought another dude in shorts.

"I could never do that, that's terrifying," is something people constantly say at parties when I mention I do cold calls for work, or stand-up comedy, or MMA. "I could never do it, what if I get hung up on/people don't laugh at me/I get punched in the face?" Yeah, it isn't a question of "if" in any of these cases.

Want to do mixed martial arts? Get ready to be punched. Want to do stand-up comedy? Get ready to bomb on stage. Want to make sales? Get ready for people to hang up on you, not get back to you, and give you a piece of their mind.

Before each of the actions you undertake, use Epictetus' advice and just consider what the experience you're about to go through will be like. Obviously, there's only so much you can know, but you can make some educated guesses. You've had a whole life of experience.

For sales, ask yourself what you're trying to make happen out of every action. What's the point of this call? What do I want my prospect to do? What do I want to say? What do they need to hear? Asking yourself this at each turn in the sales process results in far, far, far superior results than just going in and winging it. At each turn, understand and expect what is reasonable to expect. If you suspect the prospect only wants pricing to compare you to the vendor they've already selected, then don't be bent out of shape when you forward it and they don't get back.

Accept all that is involved in the process; this won't just help you make better decisions and safeguard against mistakes before you undertake any action, but it will also keep your mind steady when things inevitably do go haywire. Remember, if Zig Ziglar is right and sales is about the transfer of emotions, then it's *absolutely* necessary for the salesperson to stay the most confident and steady of anyone in the sales process. If your emotions are all over the place, nobody is going to want to buy from you.

This is probably a good time to say that I've never understood people who complain while traveling. Standing in line at passport control, the TSA, baggage claim, people huff and puff and sigh exasperatedly all the time. Yeah, it blows waiting for people who barely got a high-school degree to rifle through your stuff and move you along, but honestly, what else did you expect? Nobody, at any time flying anywhere, stopped and said "What a comfortable experience! It went exactly as smoothly as I envisioned!" Instead, travelers should expect delays, frustrations, unhelpful people, and every other manner of lame experience that comes along with schlepping from one part of the globe to another.

If you were a travel agent, the way you'd sell the frustration to a client isn't by avoiding it altogether, and letting them believe that everything is going to be smooth from start to finish, but instead by being completely upfront and realistic about it, but not by drawing undue attention to it. The same is true in all sales processes - the way to gain trust is by being honest, but not to betray a lack of confidence in the value of your product. Is it worth going through 20 hours or more of flights, passport control, and transferring in Bangkok to get to the beautiful beaches of Phuket, Thailand? If you do the right things when you get there, you bet it is.

Consider this approach when entering the serious stages of the sales process with your prospect. If you enter by letting them know what the difficult parts of the sales process will be, they'll be more likely to trust you, to stay with you while going through them, and ultimately be better served by you. Do as Epictetus instructed, and intend on keeping your mind and their mind in harmony with nature. Aim for no surprises.

Because I understood this, I tended not to be surprised by anything that happened on a cold call. Mostly I expected everything to go haywire, so if it didn't, *that* was the surprise. Once, I dialed up a VP of marketing at a major restaurant chain in the US. When she picked up the phone, I had a major surprise.

"Hello?" She said.

"Hi, Suzy Collins?" I said (names have been changed to protect the innocent).

"Um, yes?" She said.

"Hi this is Brendon calling from Scrappy Marketing Corp., did I catch you at a bad time?" There was a momentary pause as she decided whether or not she wanted to be pitched.

"Sure, you have a moment," she said, clinically.

"Sounds good - here's why I'm calling, I know you're VP of Marketing at Big Pizza Corp, and from my research it looks like you mentioned seeing mobile marketing as a growth opportunity. Well, we happen to be a mobile marketing company that does exactly what you mentioned Big Pizza was looking into doing in the recent interview you were in. Would you be open to talking about it sometime?" She paused yet again.

"You bet, here's my email, let's talk later this week. How's Thursday?" My jaw hit the floor. In my over decade of making cold calls, this is the *only* time that this has happened. Thousands upon thousands upon thousands of calls and *this one* is the only one that immediately led to a meeting right from the pitch.

Normally it goes something like this:

"This is Brendon calling from Scrappy Marketing Corp, did I catch you at a bad time?"

"Yeah Brian, I don't really have any interest," said the prospect, before having the foggiest clue what the hell he wasn't having interest in.

Or like this:

"This is Brendon calling from Scrappy Marketing Corp, did I catch you at a bad time?"

"I have a second Brendon."

"Great - I was just calling because from my research it looked like you handle the customer loyalty program at Big Brand Corp., is that right?"

"Nope, sorry Brendon, I don't."

"Oh, really? But isn't your title 'Director, Customer Loyalty Programs?'" I say, confusedly.

"Wait, yep, that's me."

-Facepalm-

And these are just the examples without expletives.

If you've been in sales for a while, you don't need me to recount to you difficult, uncomfortable, odd, or outright painful sales situations. The point, however, is this: Accepting those circumstances at the outset will equip you to move through them and keep a level head. It'll lead to more success in what you're attempting to do, and being honest with your prospect about what *they're* getting into will lead to the same. Foreseeing all these challenges will lead to greater success, both in deals closed and in comfort at work.

THE ENCHIRIDION TENET 5

Men are disturbed, not by things, but by the principles and notions which they form concerning things. Death, for instance, is not terrible, else it would have appeared so to Socrates. But the terror consists in our notion of death that it is terrible. When therefore we are hindered, or disturbed, or grieved, let us never attribute it to others, but to ourselves; that is, to our own principles. An uninstructed person will lay the fault of his own bad condition upon others. Someone just starting instruction will lay the fault on himself. Some who is perfectly instructed will place blame neither on others nor on himself.

Data is the weirdest commodity to buy.

It both exists and it doesn't exist. You can't lay your hands on it, the people who sell it say they have the best data and that every other company has the worst data. If you've ever tried to buy data or find a data partner, it's a completely exhausting exercise. Nobody in the space can tell you why their data is better or worse than anyone else's, but they'll harass you about it nonetheless.

More than one time I've gone on this great shark hunt, and each time it's been completely lame. One of the lamest parts about it are the sales guys (and it's only been guys) at each of these companies. Because their product is effectively indistinguishable from their competition, they tend to rely on high-pressure sales tactics that would be right at home on a used car lot. Each time I've been through selecting a vendor, each of these sales people from their respective organizations would call me incessantly and tell me why I would be making a bad decision if I didn't go with them. As soon as I was honest and respond "But Jake, literally all of your competition has said exactly what you just said to me, why should I listen to you?" They'd come back with a bunch of pre-arranged BS that didn't relate to anything. I always went with the cheapest option, I was never disappointed.

But because I'd gone through this exercise more than once, I began to recognize the same names from each organization. I ended up talking with all the same guys again at any new organization I moved to when it came time to evaluate a new data partner. One time, I called up a salesman from one of these big data companies.

"So, you're coming back around? Last time you made me look like a fool to my boss because I was counting on you. Are you ready to stop making bad decisions this time around?" He said as I hung up on him. Yep, ready to stop making bad decisions, which is why I hung up on him and have never spoken with him ever since. I was actually so mad I wrote an email to his manager explaining to him exactly why I wouldn't be moving ahead with their company: because this guy was a bad salesman and a jerk.

"I'm sorry Jake was offensive," his manager wrote back. Nope, he didn't get it either.

It wasn't that Jake was offensive (he was, for the record), it was that Jake misunderstood a fundamental sales principle so old that even the Stoics knew it: If a deal didn't work out, *it wasn't because of your prospect*.

"Man, I'd be a billionaire if it wasn't for all these shitty, lame prospects constantly being dumb," said a man who never made any money selling anything to anyone.

The truth is that if you didn't make a sale it's either because it's your fault or it's nobody's fault.

Many a sales manager is going to disagree with that second part, but it's true. Things either happen or they don't. If they don't happen it's either because you did something wrong, or something just went wrong.

In the case of buying data, I mostly always went with the cheapest option, because everyone looked and sounded alike, but I didn't always go with the cheapest option. The one time I didn't it was because of the salesman. On a call I told him the truth.

"Brian, I'm going to be totally forthright: every one of you data guys sounds exactly like the others. Your platforms look the same, the data looks the same, and you all say I'll be disappointed if I go with someone else, but you won't give me any good reasons why this is the case. What am I supposed to do here?" I said.

"Oh boy, yeah, that's a tough one," he said back. "How about this, what would make you trust that we're superior? Could we give you free access to the platform for your whole team for long enough to really try it?" I'd heard guys say this before, but they'd only give a week or two "free access," and that access would only be to a limited number of contacts.

"Sure," I said. "But, only having access to a limited amount of data isn't going to really show us if this is truly an improvement on our current partner or if it's better than anyone else in the marketplace."

"How long do you need?" He asked back.

"We'd need a full month, maybe six weeks," I said. He paused for a moment.

"Okay, deal - I'll send you access for your whole team, completely open, no restrictions, and you can use it to your heart's content. This will probably make my boss really mad, because I'm genuinely not supposed to do this, but why not, I think you're being honest," he responded. Moments later, before we'd even really finished the phone call, he'd already sent over our login information.

Three weeks later we signed a deal with them. This guy is still the first person I call when I need data at a new organization.

He knew that either he was to blame for a deal not working out, because he could change something and wouldn't, or the circumstances were to blame because he couldn't change something that would've needed to have been changed. In this situation, he changed what he needed to. There's no blame. There was no "sweating it." There was just a cool, clinical choice to give me what I needed to have to trust him enough to move forward with him. I hope that guy became the highest grossing salesperson that organization has ever seen, and I hope they put their loser competition out of business.

In the past, other data companies would refuse this kind of request and say things like "Sorry, if we let you have free, unfettered access to our data we'd be devaluing ourselves." Right, just like how the price of a ticket to Disney World is dependent not on how much fun you'll have there, but how few people can actually afford it. It doesn't matter which amusement park I end up going to if I think I'm going to have the same amount of fun at any of them, because I have no idea *how much fun I am going to have*. The ticket is to buy the fun, the price of the ticket has nothing to do with how much of it you're going to have. You pick the data partner to get the data and a discount on the platform doesn't affect how good the data is.

Okay, my economic arguments aside, the point is this: Epictetus is right, "When therefore we are hindered, or disturbed, or grieved, let us never attribute it to others, but to ourselves; that is, to our own principles."

We can exchange "When therefore we are hindered, or disturbed, or grieved..." with "When therefore we lose deals..." It's basically the same statement and applies exactly to sales. The fault with losing the sale comes down to "our own principles," as Epictetus would put it.

Each and every data company had principles, and each of those principles always caused me to not buy from them and go to the cheapest option. Then, one day, one salesman just didn't share that same principle. Instead, his principles said "If I have a prospect that can't tell the difference between any of his options, I'll go ahead and let him use mine for free, and he *will* see the difference." And that's why I went with him. He took *responsibility* for his side of the sale and changed what he had the power to change.

There are two kinds of entrepreneurs, of CEO's and of salespeople, so far as I can tell: The first kind gets frustrated that the marketplace is asking other things from them than they are willing to give "I can't let you have free access to our platform," or "We can't come down there and present to your whole executive team in person," or "I'm not going to drop my price point to match your last provider," and people who actually make money.

This *doesn't* mean that the customer is always right. A good way of becoming broke is to constantly slash at your margins; what this means is that if you do have the power to change something on your side of the sales equation to get the sale, fucking change it and get the sale. Understand that if it doesn't work out then, it wasn't because of anything you could've done. Write it off and go get the next one.

THE ENCHIRIDION TENET 8

Don't demand that things happen as you wish, but wish that they happen as they do happen, and you will go on well.

I developed a rule while working in a marketing-led sales development team: if marketing needs support from sales development reps (SDR) to get people to register to marketing events, everything is going to fail.

If a $60,000 dinner cruise for *free* isn't going to get people interested in coming, then a bunch of yahoos on phones and emails pitching people isn't going to budge them either. It's just the nature of the beast. The rule came together because for the better part of a year the same pattern happened: first the marketing team would commit to a big spend to host an event around an industry conference, then, the marketing team would assign huge projected attendance numbers to the event to justify their big spend. Finally, the event would be only a few days away and marketing would come running to the sales development team like the house was on fire because they didn't have enough people registered for their event. The SDR team would then have to spend a ton of time and energy bailing out the marketing team's event.

This cycle repeated itself probably twice a quarter. It was incredibly frustrating. Nobody had time to get an even keel. It's ultimately one of the reasons I quit working at this organization; they couldn't seem to ever get to a state of equilibrium. "Business as usual" was operating like an unplanned fire drill was happening.

Before you think I'm arguing against the point of Epictetus' tenet here, let me reset and explain: I recognized that things were going to continue unfolding this way, and as such, I didn't want any part in them. So I quit. I've never regretted it.

I do however regret not putting my foot down earlier when I saw the pattern from the marketing team. I saw how things were unfolding, and I should've simply said "The SDR team won't be supporting marketing events from now on. Events are here to serve to help build sales pipeline, SDR doesn't exist to support justifying a marketing spend." I didn't say this. I regret it. But, it's in the past and it's best to let go of it. That's why the rule exists for me moving forward.

Let's imagine for a moment I had done that, and we had a moment between our two teams that recognized the problem. Imagine that marketing and SDR had recognized the truth of the situation and changed their strategy. Each team would've had to come to a new understanding of how events were planned, why they were planned, and what was expected from everyone. With an agreement from both parties, if anything unexpected was to come up, we'd be able to keep an even keel because we'd both bought in. Probably, the team would've had more success, and a smoother time. But, I never did this, and we never had that moment.

Instead of accepting that things would happen as they would I decided to avoid them entirely and leave the organization. Like I said before, I've been fine with it. I sleep better at night. But, I avoided perhaps creating a valuable moment because I was afraid of how things would happen rather than wishing that things happened as they would happen.

In sales as in life, trying to control the future is a recipe for bad decision making. Being flexible, having a love of the reality as it unfolds in front of you, this leads to harmony with life and success in the position. Perhaps you have to travel for five days to four different locations, as I did early in my career. Better to accept and move with the changing flows of the river than to fight the current. The reality is whatever it happens to be.

If you continue to find yourself at half of your target numbers at the end of the month and feel shame, or guilt, or frustration, or anything, know that none of these feelings by themselves are going to cause your numbers to rise. It's not that negative feelings like those are in-and-of-themselves bad, but *reacting* to them isn't helpful. Again, a frustrated, angry, negative salesperson isn't likely going to entice anyone to buy from him.

Amor fati, the love of fate. You can't change the circumstances you're in. Whatever happened in the past to lead you here, you can't change them. But you can act in the present. You can continue to choose to act differently. When you do act, practice the act of stoic resignation and allow decisions you've made and actions you've taken to unfold as time allows. You cannot control the future in the present, you can only make the best choices you can in the moment.

A tool I use when this happens is something I developed from working at Starbucks. It's true that it isn't a sales role, it was making coffee, but it was extremely stressful. It was at the corner of State and Liberty streets in Ann Arbor, Michigan in the late aughts. It was directly across the street from the University of Michigan. At 10:30am the uncaffeinated masses, both post-class and pre-class, professors, TA's, and students all, pushed themselves into the Starbucks and demanded coffee at gunpoint. Okay, maybe not gunpoint, but that's how it felt. The line stretched to the door and outside the cafe. It was nuts. I've never felt more pressure than attempting to make four coffees at once with fifteen more behind them, all while under the piercing stares of all 19 people who were waiting. Any false move could result in spilled coffee, having to redo an order, or the worst of all: having a nineteen year-old patron yell at the top of her lungs that you ruined her caramel macchiato. Honestly, it was tough.

The first time I was caught in this situation I had a meltdown. I was pulled off the coffee machine and dozens of customers were mad. I thought I was going to get fired. In the back room, I waited for my manager to come in and ream me out for having screwed everything up. She came back, but no reaming happened.

"That was rough," she said. I nodded. "It's important that you stay calm when all of that is going on; nothing is going to result in mistakes faster than if you're overwhelmed and reacting to everything that's happening. Mistakes *will* happen, so just accept it. When they happen, remain calm and just remember that this is all over in twenty minutes no matter what happens."

That stuck with me.

"This will all be over in twenty minutes no matter what happens."

I mean, okay, fine, it might be more than twenty minutes, but still, everything is going to pass. "This too shall pass," my mother used to say to me. When I was a kid that used to drive me nuts, but as an adult, it's some of the best advice. Things will unfold as they will, and you can't do anything in the future or past; these things are outside of your control.

THE ENCHIRIDION TENETS 11 & 12

11. Never say of anything, "I have lost it"; but, "I have returned it." Is your child dead? It is returned. Is your wife dead? She is returned. Is your estate taken away? Well, and is not that likewise returned? "But he who took it away is a bad man." What difference is it to you who the giver assigns to take it back? While he gives it to you to possess, take care of it; but don't view it as your own, just as travelers view a hotel.

12. If you want to improve, reject such reasonings as these: "If I neglect my affairs, I'll have no income; if I don't correct my servant, he will be bad." For it is better to die with hunger, exempt from grief and fear, than to live in affluence with perturbation; and it is better your servant should be bad, than you unhappy.

Begin therefore from little things. Is a little oil spilt? A little wine stolen? Say to yourself, "This is the price paid for equanimity, for tranquillity, and nothing is to be had for nothing." When you call your servant, it is possible that he may not come; or, if he does, he may not do what you want. But he is by no means of such importance that it should be in his power to give you any disturbance.

Napoleon Hill is remembered for coming up with the primordial version of what, nearly a century later, become known as The Secret, which was popularized in the mid to late aughts. He purportedly learned it from Andrew Carnegie, the steel magnate. There might be something to it....

If you're not familiar, the concept of The Secret is that "thoughts are things," and "the law of attraction" causes things you think about to flow into your life. You *attract* them to you, so-to-speak. Dave Chapelle has a low-key famous joke about this that goes as follows: "Y'all ever heard of this thing called The Secret? Some white lady told me about this and I was like, 'Word?' That is the *dumbest shit I've ever heard*! Can you imagine going to a starving child in Africa and going 'No, you're doing it all wrong, you don't *want the food badly enough! Okay, imagine the ham!*'"

The guy's a savant.

Now you're going to think I went off the deep-end.

There's some truth to this, I think. Let's put the metaphysics to the side and ignore it (not a lot of profit to be made in deeply philosophical conversations), but pay attention to the core idea. To you, it *is* kind of like everything comes from the same place. "The universe," or whatever you want to call life outside yourself, sort of just manifests things into your world. Maybe they're people, maybe they're a job, who knows. This reminds me almost verbatim of the Universal Doctrine by the mythologist-cosmologist Joseph Campbell. To paraphrase, "Everything comes from one source," he says. "And to that source again must everything return."

It's where George Lucas got the idea for The Force from in Star Wars. For real.

I don't know if you're rolling your eyes or not, but I think this is actually a pretty good model for recognizing how things happen in sales. Things come from one source: phone, email, in-person, "others." And ultimately, they return. They "go away." You either make the sale, or you don't make the sale. That's it.

"Oh this is bullshit," I can hear you and your manager both saying. "So I'm just supposed to throw up my hands and let stuff happen? I'm just supposed to not do anything? What's the point of having me here?"

The good news is that probably AI is going to take your job over anyway, so this is a question you won't have to think about for much longer!

Gallows humor.

In all earnestness this is a good question, and I'll answer it this way: The first step in gaining power is recognizing where you don't have it.

As we've been over for six tenets now, you don't have the power to make decisions for others. You only have the power to act yourself. So how do you do you *influence* others to buy? It's not easy, but it's simple. Once you clear away what doesn't work you're left with only what does, and it's spoken about in Tenet 12: You treat prospects like your servants, but don't give them power to have any disturbance over you.

Prospects buy from people they like, but they also buy from people they think *are more powerful than them.*

Somewhere deep in the human brain, in the parts than run just under our level of perception, is a little mechanism that makes decisions about whether or not we think other people are more powerful than we are. That part of our brain is constantly making judgements without us knowing. "Is this person more, less, or at the same level of power and status as I am?" When this part believes that someone is less powerful than us, it cuts off how much authority we'll give that person over us.

A clear way to show you're demonstrably *less powerful* than someone is by being disturbed by them. Prospects can *feel* this, even if they aren't aware of it. This is why veteran salespeople talk about prospects playing games, bluffing, and so on.

In order to remain in a position of power and therefore authority, a salesperson must be slightly indifferent to the choices of prospects.

Years ago when I was heating up at the mobile marketing company, it was my firm belief that we were the *best* decision in mobile marketing in the marketplace *if* a marketer wanted a program that returned 10x ROI. If they truly wanted a mobile-first go-to-market strategy, any other player in the space was a mistake to partner with. That's what I ate, drank, and slept. We weren't the cheapest partner, but people got what they paid for. If someone wanted only to "check the box" for mobile marketing, we weren't the partner for them. I knew this in my bones, and because of that confidence, I was able to project a lot of power and authority into conversations with prospects.

"Well hey, I appreciate you calling, but we're about to move ahead with another partner," a marketer at a major pet supplies retailer told me.

"Oh nice, glad you see the value in mobile. Who are you moving ahead with?" I asked.

"I believe we're partnering with Big Marketing Cloud," he said. This was a division of a much larger company that bundle all kinds of additional services with their core service. They were a "box checker," for mobile.

"Let me ask you, were you in the group that made the decision to move forward with them? Can I ask, what's the reasoning for the partnership?" I asked. He paused.

"I think because they're already a partner for their other services I think, and we can get some cost savings," he said.

"Okay. So it's because they're cheap?" I asked. This question was a jab, and he could feel it. There was a momentary pause on the phone.

"Well, we thought that the best program we could create we could do with one of our current partners," he said. I knew this was factually incorrect. This was an answer he was giving on the phone, in the moment, because I pressed him and he didn't want to lose face. Maybe that's a bit bold of me to say, but I knew this simply because I knew the capabilities of the partner they were going with, I was confident he didn't do the diligence. And honestly, for him, that was okay, he wasn't the *one* responsible all the strategic decisions of their program. I also knew that because he was covering this up, he perceived me as more powerful.

"You know, is there any opportunity to speak with your team about how we're different? We have a number of current clients who decided first to go with their current cloud partner for mobile and they ended up regretting it and coming back around, only about 18 months later. Would you be open to just sharing with you why they did this and what they were unhappy about? Best to be informed," I said. He paused.

"I think we're too far down the line with our partner, sorry," he said. This is where I felt the emotion well up, I just let it pass through and roll along. This is the part that not letting the disturbance touch me was most challenging.

"Have you signed yet? It'd be best to hear what I have to share before you sign with them, at least then what I share with you can help inform the deal," I said. There was no arguing with this.

"You know, I mean," he sputtered. He was out of words. Now he was looking to bail because he couldn't say "no" anymore. "I'm not really *the* best one to share all that with."

"Okay, who is?" I asked. He told me and I had a repeat of this same conversation with two more people. Eventually, they all sat in a room and my team gave a presentation about why their money was as good as burnt if they went with our competitor and their current cloud partner. They ended up going with us; years later, the company still has their contract. Likely, if you get text messages from a pet retailer in

America, it's because of me.

None of this would've happened if I had *reacted* to what the prospects did. If I had treated the deal like I *owned it*, like it was *mine*, and not something I had never, or would never own, my emotions and reactions might've been too much and betrayed my feelings of hurt, confusion, and *lack of power*. If I had, and they had perceived it, I doubt any of them would've listened to what my team had to say, and we would've never won their business. But because I was confident, and never *reacted*, but stayed steady, I sold each prospect along the way that they could be making a mistake.

It's important to see that at any moment they could've disagreed, shut down the conversation, and closed off communication. I couldn't control those things. I didn't try to *force* them to do anything; instead only focusing on trying to communicate as effectively as possible the reality of what was *most likely* to happen with the path they had chosen based on my knowledge.

Just as travelers view a hotel, I view the deals I'm working. I take care of them, but I don't get too disturbed if something is out of place.

THE ENCHIRIDION TENET 18

When a raven happens to croak unluckily, don't allow the appearance hurry you away with it, but immediately make the distinction to yourself, and say, "None of these things are foretold to me; but either to my paltry body, or property, or reputation, or children, or wife. But to me all omens are lucky, if I will. For whichever of these things happens, it is in my control to derive advantage from it."

Years ago, I was pretty awful at dating.

I grew up playing Dungeons & Dragons, LARPing, and video games. I had trouble having *a conversation*, let alone a conversation with someone I was attracted to. Into my 20s, I was still without a girlfriend, ever. So, I decided to do something drastic and I got a dating coach.

Yep. You read that right.

I worked with a guy who at the time was rated maybe the best dating coach in the world. I figured if he couldn't help me, I might as well be celibate for life. Turns out, he was quite good, and gave me some great advice. I had all kinds of little things I did that gave away that I felt uncomfortable, and just like we covered in the last tenet, it betrayed that I wasn't powerful, and that made women I was speaking to feel uncomfortable. Thankfully, years on, I'm happily in a relationship. Apparently the advice worked.

Some of those bits of advice have stuck with me. One night we were out and I was talking to some women at a bar in Chicago when one of them did something mean. As I attempted to get a conversation going, she turned to me and put her hand in my face and loudly said "I don't date boys under six feet tall!"

Ooooph, gut punch.

I was thrown, and skulked away. I sat by myself at the bar, trying to handle the feelings of shame and inadequacy. My coach saw it and talked with me.

"I saw the whole thing," he said. "So how is sitting here wallowing helping you?"

"I don't know," I said.

"I think you do," he said. "You don't have to risk getting hurt again." He was right. "But here's the thing, you can't control if you're her type or not, only if you're *your* type or not. You can only control what you do. When women reject me like that, I choose to not care and move on."

It sounded like magic, but he went on.

"Honestly, I have a kind of self belief now that's kind of amazing. I interpret everything as valuable for me," he said. "Anything that happens, I consider it a win. Did she turn away and say she wanted to talk to her friend? Great! I know that she has a great friend who's really cool who maybe I'll meet later. Is she here with her boyfriend? Great! Here's a cool guy I can make friends with. Does she say I'm too short for her? Great! Now I know she's shallow and not to waste time for her."

This advice completely changed my life.

Not only did I start connecting with women; this changed the way I sold at the office too.

Anything that happened with a prospect I began to interpret as positive. Anything that possibly happened I found a way to spin to advantage. It did almost become magical. I simply asked myself the question "What if this were the best news I could've heard? What really, really positive thing could've happened from this?"

Whatever the answer to those questions were, I would take action on them.

Does the prospect say they already have a partner? Great! I'm glad you see the value, now I don't have to sell you on doing something vs. doing nothing. Is it not a good time to speak right now? Great! Now I can schedule a better time. Is the prospect wrapped up in a contract? Awesome! Now I know when I should reach back out and make something happen.

I began taking all feedback as positive feedback. Holy shit did it work!

It makes sense, by focusing on what is within your control, the actions you should take, and imagining everything as a positive opportunity *for you*, you basically will always take the most positive actions. Things will either work out or they won't, and if you don't act, they definitely won't. So, imagining the good things and going for them just stands to reason.

Winning over prospects is about energy, being proactive, and time management. The ability to see a pathway forward, rather than wallowing or stopping, and then taking that path, is the way to progress sales conversations. If you see things negatively, and make decisions on that negativity, you're probably going to take less action, and the actions you take won't be motivated from thinking that they'll work out. If you act without the belief that things will work out, you're likely to not make a full, serious effort. Multiply that by hundreds or even thousands of interactions throughout an entire sales career and you'll be missing out on millions of dollars of lost revenue. Que here the famous quote from Wayne Gretzky.

If Warren Buffet and Bill Gates are right, and life is just a series of little habits, then the habit to see everything in its most positive light is critical to having a good life, and making good sales.

Not only is it important to see things in their positive light, but the final point of the tenet "For whichever of these things happens, it is in my control to derive advantage from it," reminds you that *it is within your control* to derive advantage from it. It isn't *only* that "things happen," but that whether or not they're good for you *are within your power*.

Seneca, who we'll be meeting in a moment, was exiled from Rome and stripped of all his wealth. Misfortunes befell him on many sides, but writing to his mother, he stated that now, unburdened of all his "stuff" he had time to study philosophy.

In another time, in much more dire circumstances, Viktor E. Frankl, while in a concentration camp during the holocaust, wrote that he realized it was up to him to determine what the experience meant. What did it mean? What was the purpose of every moment? Frankl realized that none of the Nazi's guarding the camp could ever take away his ability to determine what this all meant, and decide how it was in his life. His decisions were his own.

It might sound a bit dire, but the point is solid: you have your choices in how to interpret something in your life. You have choices as to what you're going to do about it. You have the ability to derive value from everything.

PART THREE
SENECA

Down And Out In Rome & Sicily

Seneca, properly known as Lucius Annaeus Seneca, or Seneca The Younger (he was very young when he was born), has become a kind of quasi-deity to people in Silicon Valley startup circles. He's been lionized by writers and business people alike. Reams of machine code are wound each year to feed the interest in ebooks about him. It makes sense, he had a pretty incredible life.

The guy was from the reaches of the Roman Empire, but was from a pretty well-off family. Like most people who had any kind of ambition in the ancient world, he got involved in politics. Unfortunately, he got involved in politics during some turbulent times in the Roman Empire. The Empire was being ruled by an Emperor, and consequently there wasn't a ton of political power that senators, or any other public people, held. Still he was so smart and well spoken that he became an advisor to more than one Emperor, including the famed Caligula (who was the Donald Trump of his era), Claudius, and then Nero.

Throughout his life, Seneca received criticism from what seemed like all angles. When he was a senator, people praised him for his oratory skills. From his writing, it's pretty clear that this guy knew how to turn a phrase (oh but to have him writing email sequences!). This sometimes put him on the wrong side of the powerful people he was trying to serve. The emperor Caligula commanded Seneca to kill himself after witnessing how successful a public speaker he was. Apparently the only thing that saved Seneca is a councilor telling the idiot emperor that Seneca was sick and would probably be passing away soon anyway.

Maybe CEO's like Seneca because he's a figure that seems constantly maligned by jealous others because he's just obviously more brilliant than everyone else. Startup founders can read his writings and say to themselves "Yeah! I get it Seneca! I know what it's like for people to hate you because of how undeniably profound you are!" I digress.

As if Caligula hating him wasn't enough, a faction of jealous senators took a rumor about Seneca having an affair with a relative of Caligula's and then condemned him to death. Claudius, emperor at the time, commuted his sentence from death to exile and pushed him out of Rome. When this happened, Seneca was also mostly stripped of his possessions. From this period of time, we have a series of letters he wrote to his mom, telling her that he'll be okay. He says to her that if anything, he'll be better than okay, because now he doesn't have to worry about a bunch of asshole senators trying to mess his life up.

Not only was he exiled, but the letters to his mother indicate he had just lost a son.

It's amazing he was able to bear all of this, and not only bear it but keep a solid and positive attitude. I fall apart when my favorite bakery is out of the croissant I like in the morning.

He lived on Corsica for eight years before being recalled to Rome by the emperor Claudius, who wanted Seneca to tutor his son, the future emperor Nero. He was successful in this and prospered. Seneca actually became a successful businessman through lending money (some say forcing loans). This, yet again, garnered him a number of enemies, including the emperor Nero himself.

Eventually Nero's famously bad rule got famously bad - although many historians note that this happened *after* Nero stopped listening to Seneca's advice. A conspiracy started to kill Nero and although it is likely that Seneca wasn't a member of it, Nero ordered him to kill himself anyway. Seneca did so, cutting his veins and bleeding to death.

Such was the way life was in the ancient world. Thankfully, nobody these days besides your middle school bully orders you to kill yourself. As bad as politics is today, nobody is making other people cut their arms open in a bathtub (I wrote this at the end of Trump's first, and so far only term, we'll see what it's like when he's elected for a third time).

PASSAGE FROM MORAL LETTERS TO LUCILIUS

Besides, speech that deals with the truth should be unadorned and plain. This popular style has nothing to do with the truth; its aim is to impress the common herd, to ravish heedless ears by its speed; it does not offer itself for discussion, but snatches itself away from discussion. But how can that speech govern others which cannot itself be governed? May I not also remark that all speech which is employed for the purpose of healing our minds, ought to sink into us? Remedies do not avail unless they remain in the system.

I've known a lot of great salesmen in my life. I've been pretty lucky with a handful of good mentors who had good sales habits. Having a bad mentor can be like a rock that's impossible to get out from under. Yet again, having no mentor is pretty rough too. I digress. One of the best mentors I had was a guy named Jim Kreller. He was a veteran of the marketing technology space.

The Martech space is notorious for a few reasons. Firstly, there's a tool for goddam everything. Sometimes as a joke in a marketing technology presentation the speaker will put up a slide that displays the "Martech Ecosystem." It's just a photo of a million little screenshots of logos, because there's a billion freaking Martech companies. Secondly, marketers are notoriously dumb people. I would pump the brakes a bit here and roll back, but fuck it, let's double-down, marketers are dumb (I shouldn't be afraid of any repercussions here, marketers wouldn't read a book on sales, because why would they care about anyone selling anything!?).

Let me clarify, there are plenty of smart marketers, probably. However, most marketers are untechnical people who are working in a field that is quickly techno-fying (autocorrect hated this one). It's become increasingly important for marketers who make strategic decisions to understand how data moves around their marketing technology environment. How does information go from one platform to another? How do we track things? What does all of this data mean?

Let's remember, the people partying the latest in college were all marketing majors. Nobody gets laid because they love data.

Consequently, as new technology was created by very technical people who did *not* party into the wee hours of the morning in college, became available to help people who understand almost less-than-nothing about technology, a job emerged attempting to bridge that gap: the Martech Sales Guy.

This is who Jim Kreller was, and he was awesome at it.

Jim understood in his bones that most marketers were scared of what they didn't understand. They were terrified by complexity. They needed a strong, consistent voice to reassure them. This is what Jim embodied. He had a baritone voice that seemed to calm the whole room. He had a slow, midwest way of speaking that made anyone he conversed with want to listen. And more than that, he was a good listener. He waited until someone had totally run themselves out before he spoke. And when he did speak, he spoke in the plainest Indiana language, and never more than necessary.

Once in a meeting with a very large brand negotiating their mobile marketing contract, the prospect had received a bunch of false information about our technology from a competitor. The prospect was mad, really mad, because they'd already selected us as their preferred vendor and we were into redlining the contract together. Now, the prospect thought that everything we had was about to fall apart and if they gave us their money, we wouldn't be able to do anything we promised them. On the phone, the prospect ranted and ranted. Each time, the junior salespeople in the room wanted to step in and refute what the prospect accused us of, point-by-point. Jim kept holding his hand up as if to say "stay back, I got this." He just let the prospect talk until the guy got blue in the face (I assume, this was on a Zoom meeting). Each time the prospect finished a sentence, Jim would pause for what seemed like forever, but was probably only about five or so seconds, to see if the guy wanted to keep speaking. He did every time. This went on for an agonizing twenty minutes.

As the prospect spoke, he went through all of the bad things that were now probably going to happen as a result of this deal not working out. He described this whole nightmare scenario and was hopping mad. Finally, after about twenty minutes, the guy had talked himself out and calmed down, but still wanted answers.

"So, what do you have to say to all that?" He said, accusingly.

"Wow, that's a real nightmare scenario," Jim said.

"Yeah!" The prospect said. "What're you going to do about it."

"Nothing," Jim said. "The competitor you were speaking to told you wrong. Plain and simple."

"Well how do I know that?" Said the prospect.

"Well, I don't think you do," Jim said. "But that's why we have a clause that lets you back out of the contract in six months if you don't see this going the way you want it to. It doesn't make sense for us to think about this as a short-term relationship. You guys are a huge brand, and if we couldn't do the things we said we could, and working together went bad, we'd ruin our reputation in the marketplace. I think that's it."

The prospect paused.

"Okay that's a good point," he said. "But what guarantees do I have?"

"None, I think," Jim said back. He said it so quickly and sharply that everyone felt the tone change and everyone in the room had a laugh. "It's like anything in life. Look, I think we've made a good case as to why we can work together, and the value you're going to get out of it. I can't give you a guarantee, but I can tell you that the competitor who told you our technology would fail is just wrong."

The guy signed the contract two days later. It was one of the biggest mobile marketing deals in North America.

Salesmen use language, communication, it's our *only* tool. It really is. Yeah we *have* a product, we *have* marketing, but these things are things to *facilitate* the communication. It's the whole game. The whole shooting match. Communicating is the point.

Seneca recognized that this was also the point of philosophy. The whole thing about being a philosopher is communicating ideas. Exactly as stoics are about the rest of their lives, they should also be disciplined in their speech.

The most pertinent point to sales is the line "But how can that speech govern others which cannot itself be governed?"

How many times do we see or hear salespeople babbling on with words that offer nothing to conversation but clucking sounds? How often does that speech obscure, rather than illuminate? There are whole shadow armies of salespeople who approach their talk tracks, email copy, and intro calls like a high school essay. Everything that comes out of their mouth is the rough draft for a paper called "why you should buy from me." No wonder prospects find dealing with salespeople and considering vendors so frustrating all the freaking time.

Let's just dive into some examples of my favorite offenders:

"Hope you're having a wonderful and productive week so far. Quick intro - my name is Shawn and I am one of the founders of this company. Some background - I've started, scaled, and sold a number of companies, notably one from Y Combinator. I'm now focusing on helping online businesses like yours unlock new growth channels and scale dramatically, particularly with a new proprietary prospecting tool we built out."

Oh man, you're SO GREAT! I guess we should work with you! *eyeroll*. I love the "Quick intro -" followed only *moments* later by "Some background -". Shawn, how did you start this company while communicating so poorly? Terms like "unlock new growth channels and scale dramatically" sounds like a bunch of made up gobbledygook. He eventually *does* get around to what they do, eventually.

"I am certain that you are contacted frequently by our different channels and partners, but we are part of national business team based out of our corporate headquarters in Chicago. Would you mind pointing me in the direction of the person in charge of your network?"

This feels strangely like he did a whole dance in the first sentence. Also, who's the "we" he's talking about? Is it also the "different channels and partners"? If so, then why the hell mention them? "I'm certain a lot of people who look and sound like me get a hold of you, but we're big important people who live in a city. Who's more important than you I can talk to?" Jeez.

So many of emails that get sent are written *because someone has to write an email*. Why? Because they're trying to do their job. That's it.

Wouldn't it be wonderful if the people writing the emails or speaking on the phone were actually trying to communicate something effectively and worthwhile? This is where everyone in sales and reading is like "F-you dude, what do you know about how hard it is and what I'm trying to do everyday?" Good point. I don't. But I doubt that running on a treadmill writing emails for the sake of writing them is helping anyone either. Clear speech reveals the truth, anything else is just obscurantism.

PASSAGE FROM DE BREVITATE VITAE

It is inevitable that life will be not just very short but very miserable for those who acquire by great toil what they must keep by greater toil. They achieve what they want laboriously; they possess what they have achieved anxiously; and meanwhile they take no account of time that will never more return. New preoccupations take the place of the old, hope excites more hope and ambition more ambition. They do not look for an end to their misery, but simply change the reason for it.

There's an old Calvin & Hobbes cartoon I'm fond of. In it, young Calvin goes through a terrible day at school, and everything goes wrong. Exasperatedly, he makes it home, only to be yelled at by his parents. Finally, as he goes to bed, his mother tucks him in and says "tomorrow's another big day."

People always say things like "It's about the journey, not the destination." I always roll my eyes and think, "I mean, it's also *kind of* about the destination." However, point taken, you can't hate where you are in the present *all the time*. Whatever is happening now is happening forever.

This line from On The Shortness of Life cuts through me: "They achieve what they want laboriously; they possess what they have achieved anxiously." To anyone who buys into the idea that you have to work harder than everyone else to achieve what you want, this should terrify you. If you only ever have to outwork, overwork, and outlast everyone to succeed, then you're getting onto a treadmill you'll never be able to get off of. It isn't so much that nobody should ever work hard at something, or that all work that is hard should necessarily be enjoyable, but more so recognizing that there *is* a trap there.

Sales is a job that you can easily burn out on. That same amazing manager, Jim Kreller, would cap people at 54 hours a week. Some people are going to read that and think "Woah!? 54 hours a week that's insane! I can't believe someone would work *that much*," and some salespeople are going to read that and think "Ooooph, I do 55 *every* week."

Indeed, when I first got into being an account executive I worked in international sales. My day started sometimes at five in the morning with calls to the UK, France, and Germany, then ended at 10pm with calls to New Zealand, Japan, and Australia the next day. It was super, duper rough. In addition to days like that I would often travel sometimes for days on end with only a few hours of sleep before I had to get up and take another flight, rent a car, and get right back to work. I was in my mid-20s, but woah, it was rough.

I worked with a guy who became my unofficial older brother he was such a good mentor, a guy named Rod Bolls. This guy did nine Iron Mans and ran the Leadville100, a hundred mile ultramarathon that takes place entirely over 10,000 feet of elevation. He built more than one multi-million dollar company in his life. He would always tell me to take it easy, "It's about balance," he'd say. For the longest time, I never knew what this meant. "You need recovery time, you don't want to *push* yourself, you just want to do the hard things." This kind of talk was cryptic and made no sense to me. I'd constantly be getting sick, working myself until I'd pass out and burn out.

Not only would I get sick, but I'd constantly run myself ragged with challenging and difficult prospects who wanted to make me jump through all kinds of hoops for them. "Why don't you try to find easier people to deal with? For this much work you could be selling tons more," Rod would say. I totally didn't get what he meant. I ran myself ragged for years and finally quit working at the job because I was burned out. I barely sold anything, I felt like a total failure. It took me years more to learn to sell, but the lesson finally hit me: There are good prospects and there are bad prospects, don't waste time with bad ones.

For all the time you're spending with bad prospects, you could be spending time with good ones. I didn't put two and two together for some reason back then, but Seneca did thousands of years ago: Don't waste your time on things that will cause you more trouble than they're worth. When it comes to sales, fire bad prospects.

Looking back on it, Rod would handle this situation by cutting straight into how serious the prospect was. He'd even ask it like that "Let me ask you, are you serious? How serious are you about using us as an option?" At the time I was too gun-shy to say this. Looking back now, if I had just known how much time I would've wasted by attempting to win over prospects who weren't serious or weren't ready, I could've had not one but two successful sales careers, rather than one mediocre one.

This is exactly the point that Seneca is making though. It's not that nothing is worth working hard for, it's that working hard for things that take more work to keep is just robbing all your time away. The lesson every veteran salesperson knows intimately is that much of time, things don't work out. Consequently, the best salespeople qualify hard and are realistic about the likelihood of something *not* working out.

Rod also did another thing that the best salespeople do: He saw the work, the process, as fun. He really enjoyed the whole thing. Negotiation, prospecting, cold emails, leveraging his network, even traveling for work was all fun for him. There was no "off time." I mean, he took time off, but he even saw that as part of a grand whole of his life. He was a business development, sales guy, he was an entrepreneur, he was an athlete. All of it was one big thing.

Look at the way that Seneca phrases it, "New preoccupations take the place of the old, hope excites more hope and ambition more ambition. They do not look for an end to their misery, but simply change the reason for it."

People who find the joy in the work are the ones who reach the highest levels of success. "I fell in love with the work," Jerry Seinfeld said when asked how he became such a prolific comedian. There's no guarantee any of your work will go anywhere, or mean anything, but if you love doing it, and it happens to pay, then that's where you'll make your fortune.

For me, I started to experience success when I got into a flow state while prospecting. I started feeling joy when listening to music and making cold calls, getting excited to come up with new and creative ways to write emails. I started really enjoying listening, and having fun building rapport with prospects on the phone. In short, I found things to like. Soon, the annoying part of the job became different things. That's actually how you know you're leveling up and improving, when the former annoying things become enjoyable and then there are new things that feel like work.

The key is to find the love for the job in the work, then continue in a way that's always enjoyable. Yeah, this isn't easy, but it isn't hard either. You're just deciding to do it, and then doing it. Work well for good prospects, work well for yourself, and don't get bent out of shape by anything. You'll probably end up owning the place.

The trap you don't want to get caught in is what I call the "All the friends of my parents" trap. Growing up, my parents used to like to have all kinds of parties. My mom and dad were well liked and had a pretty big group of friends. They'd throw different parties throughout the year and our house was like a hotel lobby; people came in an out, and it was normal to see lots of familiar faces. Honestly, it was a pretty great way to grow up because I got to get to know a lot of grown-ups and hear their thoughts about all kinds of things. Over an over though, I heard a familiar chorus.

One of my parents' friends would talk about wanting something, maybe it was a sports car, maybe it was a boat, maybe it was some land on one of the Great Lakes. For some of them, it was as ambitious as a vineyard. The refrain was the same though: for weeks or months or years I would hear about the thing they wanted. Then one day, they got that thing. Then I would only ever hear about all the problems with that thing.

"Oh man, the car/boat is back in the shop."

"I'm up there like every weekend trying to get the ground right for the vines again this season."

"Nearly half of my budget goes to paying for labor for the harvest time, it's crazy."

It's one thing to find something you love that requires all your time, but it always felt like my all my parents' friends fell into a trap: There's an X, that X will make me happy, so I'm going to work for that X. Then, they'd get the X and they wouldn't really be any happier than before, but now they had a whole bunch of work to maintain the X.

The stoic's pathway to joy is the same: keep what makes you joyful within your locus of control. The smaller it is, the less it requires, the more available it happens to be, the more you'll have it. This is why all the best salesmen and saleswomen I've known were always cool as a cucumber nearly all the time. Any setbacks, anything that would make your humble narrator lose his mind, those great salespeople not only took in stride but acted almost as if those obstacles were the *reason* for the walk.

I'd probably be a millionaire if I had used the time I spent chasing bad deals on just reasonably developing good ones, or looking for more good ones.

A simple solution to ending this conundrum comes from stoic philosophy itself: Just think through what getting the thing you want is going to take, and what it's going to be like after you get it (or if you don't - eek!). I normally do this by taking out a notebook and writing down what getting the thing would look like. How much is it going to require of me? What is my pathway going to look like? How would I get it? Then imagine yourself getting it. Feel all the good parts. Okay, now write about what having it would be like. Get all the good parts out of yourself. Sure, you'd achieved it, now what? Sometimes, after I write all the good things I literally draw a line on the page and under it I write "okay, now all the bad stuff." Then I write down everything that's awful about what getting the thing you want will be like. Really go for broke here.

After I have a good long list in both camps, I always write down "Okay, so what will *probably* happen?" Then I write down all of this. What's the most likely thing to happen, given what I know about life, how things tend to go, and knowledge of myself? This is where I have to be careful about being too positive.

Now you have a full picture about what you're getting into. Now you know what everything is likely going to look like, and how it's going to affect your life. Of course, surprises can come up, this isn't a totally exhaustive list, but you're better informed than having not done it. Also, when you do encounter difficulty, frustration, or other problems with your toil, you can reflect and go "Yep, this was all a part of the plan."

PART FOUR
MARCUS AURELIUS

The Ancient World's CEO

Many of us imagine what it would be like running a big organization. We imagine ourselves working in some big building, looking at computer screens and having subordinates deliver reports to us about how such-and-such a thing is doing. In many ways, Marcus Aurelius was the first "CEO" as we would recognize it today, except he did it without any computers, no cell-phones, and no PR department.

Marcus was emperor of the largest empire the world had ever seen to that point for about 20 years. Millions of people lived and died under his auspices. Every day, decisions he made affected the lives of everyone in the Roman empire. According to some beliefs, he was anointed a living god in the tradition of Caesars before him. Imagine the pressure. You think your team puts pressure on you? Imagine if they thought you were a living deity.

In these days we value data & numbers to make decisions; in Marcus' time, data & numbers were almost non-existent (plus, all the numbers looked like letters anyway). Instead, like the world of the book Dune, Marcus Aurelius had to rely only on the testimony of all the people around him. Unless he went somewhere and saw it firsthand (which he did, quite often), he had to trust that what people were telling him was in fact accurate.

Imagine the confusion, the difficulty, the disconnectedness of the world he inhabited. Without the assistance of technology to help run the empire, he was at the mercy of however effective or ineffective the people around him were. One character flaw in himself or his advisors could lead to decisions that cost lives. People did in fact die, as his reign was fraught with war on nearly all fronts. He fought wars against Germanic barbarians, against the Parthian empire, and a "war" against an outbreak of plague that killed upwards of five million

Romans.

Luckily for the people in his empire, and for us, Marcus had a teacher that greatly influenced him in his youth toward a stoic state of mind. Beginning in about 170AD, the emperor began writing little letters and musings to himself while on campaign, much like people do today. In them, he would write small reminders about how to keep a stoic outlook. He did this for 10 years.

At some point, these personal musings and notes were collected and published under a handful of different names. Sometimes called "To Himself", sometimes "Things to One's Self", but the name that it's come down to us by is "Meditations."

What we have in Meditations is a window in time and space, back to the insights, temperament, and character of perhaps the most powerful man in the world. This work has been appreciated by powerful people throughout the prevailing two millennia since it was written. Lovers of it have included a group of people who have varied in every other character trait but one: they've all occupied powerful positions. From Frederick the Great of Prussia, to John Stewart Mill, to former Chinese Premier Wen Jiabao to Bill Clinton, even retired American general James Mattis is said to have carried a copy of Meditations with him while on deployment.

When everything seems overwhelming, the whole world seems out of control, and you have no idea what to do, Meditations is a powerful refuge. I myself return to it again and again. When attempting to do anything in life that involve struggle with others even if that other is somehow yourself, it offers advice that calms and focuses.

PASSAGE FROM BOOK II

When you wake up in the morning, tell yourself: The people I deal with today will be meddling, ungrateful, arrogant, dishonest, jealous, and surly. They are like this because they can't tell good from evil.

How do you exist in a world without "data" as we understand it today? You have only one real option: trust the people around you. Someone has to see it, hear it, touch it, smell it, and then report it back to you. There is no video. There are no photographs. There are no data.

In this kind of world, people are the lynchpin to everything.

Truthfully, it isn't *that* much different than the world we're in today, we just have the illusion that things aren't quite as dependent on people because of all this externalized "stuff." It makes sense, and in many ways the world *isn't* as dependent directly upon others (traffic, for example is regulated by lights and not people, as it was for all-time before the traffic light), but predominantly the world is almost the same as it was two thousand years ago.

When Marcus Aurelius was mobilizing legions for war in Germania he was completely reliant upon the buy-in of people all along the way. From his generals all the way down to the individual legionaries, he needed all of them to be sold on their purpose. Nobody could check a smartphone to see where the army was. Nobody got to watch video of atrocities the enemy had committed to know why they were fighting. Nobody even *knew* for a fact where orders they received were issued from - today, the president would make a statement on video and send it.

In this world of people, everyone has an agenda. One valuable part of living in a world where some things have been "outsourced" to technology is that we don't have to calculate the agenda of what the technology is doing (we'll see how long this lasts). In a world of people, everyone has an agenda, and everyone is fallible.

Marcus Aurelius dealt with this every single day, and so do you.

In sales, your job *is* people.

Whether you make a sale or not, whether you make your numbers or not, whether your product or service takes over the marketplace or becomes completely useless is entirely up to people. Nobody buys because a machine tells them to.

Because your world is so based upon the whims of others, let's make sure you base your strategies for dealing with others on reason. This is why I love Marcus Aurelius' approach so much here: He remind himself whenever he wrote this that all the people he deals with are all basically awful. They're probably not trustworthy, and they're not honest, and they're selfish, and they're going to try and ruin his plans. This isn't *because* they're evil, but instead because they can't tell the difference *between* good and evil.

Remember the passage from Epictetus about going to the bath? He asks us to recall what going to the bath is like. He reminds us that the bath is noisy, is filled with idiots, and you won't really get any rest or relaxation. This way, Epictetus says it, "You can keep yourself in harmony with the nature of things." This leads to you making better decisions about the bath, when you go, what you're going to do, and you won't be frustrated and disappointed because you've accustomed yourself to what it's really going to be like. In this passage, Marcus Aurelius is doing *the same thing*, but with people.

What's important to keep in mind about this too is that he was Emperor of Rome; the most powerful man in the known world, and someone that nobody but nobody wanted to displease. *However*, even he knew not to expect the best from everyone around him. If he dealt with BS from people all the time, how are you supposed to be any different?

In sales, in life, it's important to get an accurate view of the path ahead. It becomes much easier to make good, effective decision when considering the reality of what could possibly go wrong. I see it time and time again with new salespeople on my team. They'll rely on someone else, a prospect, a referrer, even a colleague, for *anything*, only to see that person fail them. It isn't out of malice. It isn't out of kniving, or some other direct *evil*. Instead, it's out of a more mundane, banal evil: incompetence, or simply the myopic blindness to others that comes with self interest.

Most people are *accurately* interested only in themselves. As a result, they think only in the limited terms of their own well being. A leader like Aurelius understood that building a vision *requires* selling people and *requires* meeting them where they're at and planning for it. How does this work in sales? A few ways.

Firstly, when dealing with prospects, it is *always* best to sell to people *in terms* of their own interest. I have a phrase, "Play the man, not the position." It might be the person you're speaking with's job to evaluate your product, but just because it's their function doesn't mean they're not a person themselves. The way Rod Bolls used to say this was "You've got to make it easy for the guy to say yes to you." Why is it in *their* best interest to work with you? Sell to *them*. Once they've bought in to why it's good for them, their self-interest will keep them on your agenda.

The way you do this is the same way someone in Marcus' time did it: practice good listening skills. Listen when in conversation with a prospect but don't stop there. Listen to the organization. What content is the prospect's company putting into the marketplace? Did the prospect post anything on LinkedIn to indicate where their head is at? Listen for clues on how to position your product or service as a solution *to them*, not just to their job or to their organization.

That's the other way I like to think about it "Get your agenda on their agenda." That's it, that's sales. That's the whole ball game. If you can do *that* you're the greatest salesman on the planet and nothing will stop you. How can you make what you want to do so super sweet to *them* that they change their plans for it? That's sales. Marcus Aurelius reminds us that their self interest, and devotion to the banal evils that we all fall prey to, is a resource we can count on. I once recommended a friend of mine hire an outsourced sales company because I knew I'd get a good commission on the referral. Sure, they did good work, but that's not *why* I recommended it. This is to say, don't bribe people, that's wrong, but do recognize that people make decisions in their best interest. Figure out how to appeal to that and you'll win everyone over.

Secondly, recognize that even *if* you have people on board with you, they could easily still do something dastardly to ruin your plans. In fact, count on it. Once again, the sales master Rod Bolls used to say "You gotta plan for people to fuck shit up." Sitting in his office, he'd sometimes think out loud about how a deal was going to get closed.

He'd stare at his whiteboard and then rattle off three, four, sometimes five or more ways that something could go wrong. Then he'd draw out how each of those things were going to happen, and his counter-plan for each of them. Honestly, it was astounding.

Most of the time when Rod did this, he'd name off really lame and mundane sounding things that I wouldn't consider: "He's going to get the contract and sit on it, then forget about it. He's going to see our competitor then suddenly want us to rebid against their bid. He's going to want to choose between us and going on another vacation." Rod would map out all of these things and what to do to combat the most boring of potential derailments. And it worked, Rod Bolls was so good at sales he created a company that employs dozens of people and makes tons of money. The guy knew what he was doing, and it was all because he counted on people to "fuck shit up."

Remember that the focus of stoic philosophy is founding the well-being of your life on only what you can control. What Rod was doing with these moments of planning was basically asking himself "What can I do that might mitigate any of these turns of events?" Maybe it works out, maybe it doesn't, but the attempt will *more likely* result in things working out than doing nothing. Quite simply, Marcus Aurelius' method of recognizing that *people* are the weak spot because they're weak is critical to making your own plans on how to overcome their weaknesses.

Finally, Marcus' thoughts are important for us and our mental health. Truly, people don't always do their best work. People fail. People are dicks and jerks. Even us. They're not doing it out of evil, but because they don't really understand the difference between good and evil. They're ignorant at best. Even we're prone to this. While Marcus doesn't say "forgive them," he does recognize that this is just their nature. It's our nature too. Each of us. So, recognize that you'll be susceptible to this kind of behavior too and maybe cut yourself a little slack, and plan for it.

Wake up in the morning and remind yourself of this point and see what kind of day you have. You'll probably be pleasantly surprised by people who rise to the occasion, and not disturbed when people act like the everyday mundane jerks and idiots we all are. You might even find it in your heart to forgive yourself when you don't do your best.

PASSAGE FROM BOOK V

In a sense, people are our proper occupation. Our job is to do them good and put up with them. But when they obstruct our proper tasks, they become irrelevant to us--like sun, wind, and animals. Our actions may be impeded by them, but there can be no impeding our intentions or our dispositions. Because we can accommodate and adapt. The mind adapts and converts to its own purposes the obstacle to our acting. The impediment to action advances action. What stands in the way becomes the way.

One of my favorite saying is "Art from adversity." The meaning is clear: obstacles become moments of inspiration. Another famous author (did this guy just refer to himself as "famous"?) said it this way: The obstacle is the way.

Maybe those things are true, maybe they're not. Maybe the obstacle is the way you should go, maybe it's just an obstacle and it would've made more sense to go around. Maybe adversity causes inspiration, maybe it doesn't and it's just an annoying constraint; the harpsichord wasn't a *better* instrument because it had a more limited range than the piano, otherwise there would've been no reason to invent the piano.

What I do know is that in life, anything you're trying to do is going to encounter obstacles and impediments; the *wrong* thing to do is let yourself become disturbed by any of these obstacles. Especially when these obstacles become people.

So, if any former history majors are reading this, prepare to roll your eyes. Within the same few decades two major, world-history-shaking revolutions took place: The American, and the French. The two are admittedly so qualitatively different that comparing them does, in fact, become ridiculous, especially in this book. Nevertheless, I shall, as the impediment to action advances action and what stands in the way becomes the way (see what I did there? This is why I'm "famous").

Two groups of people were angry that traditional structures of social order were impeding their upward mobility: American colonists and the "third estate" of French society. Each group was fueled with revolutionary fervor, informed by enlightenment thoughts that heretofore nobody had had before. Governments exist at the consent of the people? The point of government is the advancement of the public good? The individual is the most atomic part of the social order? On two continents, these ideas provided a kindling to thoughts of revolution.

In America, the idea was one of balancing *imperfect* social forces against one another. In essence, when one group of people want A to happen, but another want B to happen, group B becomes an obstruction and impediment to group A. Instead of letting this antagonism die on the vine, or lead to a disillusionment of the social order that both groups are participating in, the framers of the American system of government provided all kinds of institutional checks and balances. What this meant for history is that different groups of people who have completely different world views could disagree *but still participate*. There was no need of a certain kind of American Citizen. No one type of citizen needed to exist.

This American system, and its inclusion of all of the flaws of the people within it, and how much they would be impediments and obstacles to one another, yet could still participate together, was so effective that it only really broke down *once* in its nearly 250 life. It was the American Civil War that caused the biggest and most bitter disagreement; and that disagreement *was in fact* about the foundational principles of government: who should be included. Among other reasons, the *raison d'être* of the confederate states was to preserve the institution of slavery. In effect, what the American system finally said, nearly 100 years after its founding was "Yes, ALL people get to participate, no matter what they look like."

Was it perfect? No. Is it perfect? No. *Does perfection matter to the proper functioning of the United States?* No. Do we want it to be perfect? No, because the framers of the American system of government *counted* on people being obstacles and impediments to one another and made it a feature, not a bug.

The American Constitution was ratified amongst the states in September of 1787. Truly, it was a day worth remembering in the world. Eighteen months later the French Revolution began with a meeting of the Estates-General of 1789, three months later a mob stormed the Bastille in Paris and The Marquis de Lafayette, hero of the American Revolution, took of command of the National Guard to establish order. Within the month, peasants across France armed themselves and began attacking and looting homes of the nobility, La Grande Peur, The Great Fear, had begun. In the remaining months of 1789 the revolutionaries would abolish the feudal system which had existed for nearly a millenia in France, pass the Declaration of the Rights of Man and of the Citizen, influenced by the writer of the American Declaration of Independence, Thomas Jefferson.

From its inception, there was a great fear amongst the revolutionaries that monarchists in their ranks would undermine the project of the revolution. So many wealthy, landed noble families had so much to lose. King Louis and the royal family were brought under arrest after they were caught trying to flee the country. France was attacked on all sides by neighboring powers. The whole project of the rights of man, of self-determination, and revolutionary thought was threatened. Revolutionary leaders formed The Committee for Public Safety in 1791. It's purpose, to purge the revolution of unsavory elements. Here is where the wheel turned: people who disagreed were now an object, an impediment to the revolution. If these people couldn't be won over, they'd be eliminated.

Six years and four months since the American Constitution was adopted, the French Revolution executed their former monarch, King Louis, in Place de la Concorde, Paris. This clarion call heralded only more to come. In the following year, 1793, The Reign of Terror gripped revolutionary France. Paranoia and frothing determination to see the project of the revolution to its glorious conclusion released upon the French people a plague year of death. Between when it began in May of 1793 and when it ended in July of 1794, when the manic conductor of The Terror, Maximilian Robespierre, finally felt the cold slice of the guillotine, nearly 17,000 French men and women had been executed. Of them, more than 2,600 in Paris alone. Across the French nation, in one year, it was nearly 45 people per day executed because they were "obstacles" and "impediments."

Now here's the part that's basically reductio ad absurdum: In America, it was planned that the flaws of all people were to be included, and *a part of the system*. In America, the point was antagonism, obstruction, and impediment. That *was the way*. And the only time it broke down is when American's disagreed over the definition of "people." In France, this was not the case. There *was a revolutionary project*. That project was to liberate and empower man to become his most illustrious self. Anyone who disagreed with that became an obstacle to be removed.

So what the fuck does this have to do with sales? Good question. I'm not really sure, but it's a cool story.

Here's how it applies: In sales, people are you job, your work. And just like in the American system, their objections, impediments, and obstruction are a feature, not a bug.

Early in my career I had a call with a prospect. Sitting in the office with Rodney Bolls, I spoke on the phone to a guy who wanted to buy containers, which is what we were selling at the time. This guy was interested, but he had never bought containers and he wasn't sure if he could trust us or the product yet. As we talked, he expressed his interest and his misgivings, and I wasn't sure what to do, so we concluded the call.

"What's going on?" Rod shot over.

"Well, this guy wants to buy but he isn't really sure about our product because he's never seen it, or anything," I said.

"How much is he going to buy?" Rod asked.

"Could be a few orders, he's still working it out," I said.

"Get that guy back on the phone!" Rod exclaimed.

I dialed him back up.

"Hey! This is Rod Bolls, I'm Brendon's parole officer," he joked. "Here's the deal, how ready are you to buy?" The guy explained that he had a plan and knew he wanted to do something.

"Okay, we're going to send a container out to you so you can see it in person, Brendon is going to be there on the ground to show it to you. How's Friday next week? Only thing, you've got to be ready to sign there if you like it."

The guy agreed to all of it. A week later I was on the ground with the container talking to the guy. Rod had gotten it done in minutes. I wasn't sure what to do with the obstacles, Rod was immediately sure what to do with the obstacle.

In sales, obstacles happen all the time. The whole damn thing is obstacles. People hang up on cold calls, people forget to reply to emails, people forget to show up for demos, people argue over payment terms. The entire career of sales is dealing with people as obstacles, and you have a choice: do you refuse the obstacle and thereby refuse the person? Or do you embrace the obstacle, and thereby embrace the person?

I was refused as a person once.

Every time I take the helm of a sales team, the same thing happens: we have to find a new data partner. If you, dear reader, have ever been through this grind before, you have my sympathy. In the mid 2010s, every data provider looked and sounded the same.

"We have a great platform that has great data vetted by our unique system," is what every single one of them would say. Every. Single. One.

Nobody said anything different, and to make it worse, they all shat on one another all the time.

"Oh are you talking to DataCloud? Let me tell you about how bad their data is!"

"Don't compare us to OrgDiscovery, we're really not on the same level at all, they're honestly garbage, you might as well buy your data from Craigslist."

"Are you thinking about InfoRace? They're the worst, stupidest, most backward & butt-headed data platform on the internet, go with us!"

What's ironic in retrospect is that every single one of those data platforms ended up purchased and lumped together. Hilarious.

In any case, the data platform consideration process was ridiculous. You can't know the quality of product you can't try, and every time I asked for each platform to line up the data on a mirror and give us a taste, they wouldn't budge. Legit, every single one of them wanted us to sign a year-long contract without so much as testing them out. Everything started to smell like BS.

Finally, on a call with a rep I said "look, either give us some access to test your data or this will be our last call." Now the rep had a choice: either trust me, give me access to some of the data I wanted to try, or double-down on being a nightclub bouncer and keeping me out. If his boss had been Rodney Bolls, you, reader, and I both know what he would've done. But Rod wasn't his boss, a total douche was his boss.

"You know Brendon, you're going to be really sorry you didn't go with us when -" I cut him off there and didn't let him finish. Nobody but nobody tells me I'm going to be "sorry" for not doing business with him.

"YOU are going to be sorry you tried this strong-arm tactic on me!" I hung up the phone on him. Minutes later I got another phone call. I picked it up. It was the CRO of the company I had just hung up on.

"So, Mr. Lemon, is there anything we can do to convince you to go with us?" He said.

"What you *could've* done is given me some access to some data to get a sense of how much quality your product has. Even my drug dealer would do that. And you *could've* employed someone who wasn't a dick on the phone. Now I'm going to work with one of your competitors, because I don't get into bed with companies who employ the kind of people you do. Goodbye." I hung up on him too. I really said those things. Find someone from my office circa 2016 and they'll confirm it.

That is what happens when a salesperson treats a prospect like an obstacle, rather than an opportunity to advance action. I went with a competitor. The competitor was totally fine, I've never looked back, I was never sorry.

Later, that rep died in a bar fight with a grizzly bear.

Okay, that didn't happen, but it would've been a poetic end for a guy who was a total jerk.

"The impediment to action advances action."

Another way to say "Art from adversity" is "Necessity is the mother of all creation."

At a major digital marketing firm I worked at, we never had any sales tools. Time after time we'd get on the phone with a prospect and they'd ask to see our platform, and we couldn't show it to them. Mostly, we couldn't show it because it looked awful. But we also couldn't show it because there was a company policy against it. Normally, this isn't that big of a deal, we'd show someone a video, or a slide deck, or something else that would give someone an idea of what the product or solution looks like. However, at this company, nothing like this existed.

I barked up the chain about how we needed this sales resource and the answer came back "Great! We'll put one together for you soon." I was excited; my reps were asking for a tool to show the platform, and now we'd be getting one. This was in July of that year. By November, we'd given up on seeing anything.

Meeting after meeting with my team was the same; "How come we don't have the video yet? We have people who want to see it but don't want to move forward with us until they do." It was frustrating.

In one meeting with the executive team I brought it up again. "Oh, we have to tell you - there's actually been some shuffling around the sales enablement and marketing teams. That project is going to take another month to sort out I think." That was it, five months was enough. Likely, because I'd heard this song-and-dance before, it would take another five months until we saw something.

That day I went online and searched for some screen recording and hosting software, downloaded it, and put my own deck together. I recorded a presentation myself and showed my team the next day. Apparently I'd just beaten my own team to the punch; two members of my team showed me a deck they'd put together themselves in that same meeting. Those same two guys got promoted within the year. The impediment to action becomes the impetus to action.

Salespeople who embrace this thrive and succeed. Salespeople who reject it fail. It's that simple.

People are your job in sales. Embracing people, building rapport and earning trust is why they buy. If people make themselves an obstacle, you *must* embrace them, that's the only way a sale is going to be made. Rejecting prospects never led to anyone selling anything. Instead of getting sour grapes and blaming your prospects, overcome and adapt. That's the challenge of sales. That is the paradox. That *is* the job.

PART FIVE
CONCLUSION

So What's This All Mean?

The game of sales is won by a paradoxical and sometimes conflicting set of principles and actions. When selling, sometimes it serves to push and push hard, sometimes a light touch serves, sometimes aggressive action wins the prospect, other times, patience. In some ways, a successful salesperson has to be like a master of Bruce Lee's Jeet Kune Do; able to flexibly switch from one effective method to another, depending on circumstance.

This makes sense, because sales is really a lot of chaos.

Really, the world is just chaos. Probably, there's no great ordering function to any of it. Maybe there is, who knows. What I do know is that waking up every day and confronting the world of chaos takes the heart of a hero.

The daily battle, the slog, the constant unknown, can be a crushing force. It can be exhausting. Many good people I've known in sales, including myself, can burn out by trying to run as hard as they can at the switch every day. The world of sales will always take what you're going to give it, and won't always give back. Such is the nature of the chaos of the profession.

What stoicism can give you is a sense of self control and calm rarely experienced in the modern world. Cell phones, computers, presentations, emails, hundreds of passwords, SaaS, enablement platforms, cloud computing, hundreds and hundreds of bits of software that will help you solve for XYZ. It's almost like our whole social order wholesale decided to pretend that everything is achievable for everyone. It isn't.

In a world that constantly pushes the line on you that *you* are responsible for your lot in life, you and you alone, and that *you* have control over your fate, perhaps the most radical thing to do is admit when you don't.

Every day, way more things happen that affect us that are outside of our control than we can possibly respond to properly. In this world, success is as accidental as failure. This doesn't mean throwing up our hands and abdicating any ambition or action, but it does mean not being disturbed when the world decides to go another way. You can't control the weather, so it doesn't make sense to get worked up over it.

The three stoics in this book went through amazingly difficult times in a world that was harshly indifferent to any of their desires. They knew they didn't control much about their lives, but chose to act anyway, and achieve great things. You can do the same.

I hope you've enjoyed reading this book, it was for me as much as for you. I need to hear these lessons too... daily.

www.ingramcontent.com/pod-product-compliance
Lightning Source LLC
Chambersburg PA
CBHW051735040426
42447CB00008B/1148